POKER:
THE REAL DEAL

BY PHIL GORDON AND JONATHAN GROTENSTEIN

SSE

SIMON SPOTLIGHT ENTERTAINMENT
New York London Toronto Sydney

SIMON SPOTLIGHT ENTERTAINMENT

An imprint of Simon & Schuster Children's Publishing Division

1230 Avenue of the Americas, New York, New York 10020

SIMON SPOTLIGHT ENTERTAINMENT

and related logo are trademarks of Simon & Schuster, Inc.

Design and Typography: Interrobang Design Studio

Manufactured in the United States of America

First Edition 10 9 8 7 6 5 4 3

Library of Congress Control Number 2004011656

ISBN 0-689-87590-8

DEDICATION

This work is dedicated to the wonderful woman who taught me to play poker and much, much more, my great-aunt, Marie "Lib" Elizabeth Lucas. Although she can no longer call "five-card draw, nothing wild except the dealer," her memory is with me in every tournament and every side game.

In our last poker game, just a week before she died, Lib beat me out of a $1.50 pot. She gleefully turned over what was a stone cold bluff, and then proceeded to tell the entire wing of the hospital that she had taken me for my last dollar. With Lib, the pots weren't big, but the lessons and love were huge.

Lib died of cancer just a few hours before I won the professional division of the World Poker Tour's Aruba tournament in October 2002. I am donating a portion of the proceeds from this work and all of my poker tournament successes to the Cancer Research and Prevention Foundation (www.preventcancer.org) in her honor.

"See, I have this picture in my head. Me sitting at the big table, Doyle Brunson on my left, Amarillo Slim to my right, playing in the World Series of Poker . . ."
— MATT DAMON AS MIKE McDERMOTT, *Rounders*

ACKNOWLEDGMENTS

PHIL GORDON

I would like to thank all the Tiltboys (Rafe Furst, Dave "Diceboy" Lambert, Steve Miranda, Perry Friedman, Paul Swiencicki, Tony Glenning, Kim Scheinberg, John Kullman, Josh Paley, Michael Stern, Lenny Augustine, Bruce Hayek, Russ Garber) for fifteen years of poker fun. Wednesday night, Tiltboy Poker Night, is still the best night of the week. The games of "Spit-and-Shit Ding-a-Ling-with-a-Twist" will always be among my favorite poker memories.

Of course, my friends and family have played a great role in everything—Mom, Dad, and step-mom Ann, sister Ashley and brother-in-law Ryan, nephew Zakai and niece Anisa, Barb Smith, Rick Averitt, my grandmother Martha Lucas, and Shelby Driggers. I'm also incredibly proud of my godchildren: Ben Philip Leader, Quinn and Savannah Averitt, Winnie Philana, and Charlie Swiencicki. Thank you all for your love and support.

My best friend, Rafe Furst, deserves an entire chapter of dedication himself. We lived together for more than a year in a thirty-six-foot RV, traveling forty-two thousand miles around the country playing poker and going to sporting events. The trip we dubbed "The Ultimate Sports Adventure" was the best year of my life. Check out more than five thousand pictures and stories from the greatest road trip in sports history at *www.ultimatesportsadventure.com.*

In business, you need people who you can trust. I am very lucky to have some incredibly talented people on my side: my agent Jay Srinivasan, my PR guys Jack Glasure and the Glasure Group, the folks at NTN, and collaborators Luke Lincoln, P. J. O'Neil, and Brian Efird. Thank you all for your hard work and friendship.

In every poker player's life, there are people who have brought you along, sharing their knowledge, secrets, and experiences. My friends at FullTiltPoker.com are without doubt the best players in the world. Their tutelage and friendship is, in large part, responsible for my success in poker. Chris "Jesus" Ferguson, Howard Lederer, Phil Ivey, John Juanda, Eric Seidel, Erick Lindgren, and Andy Bloch are always willing to talk about hands, rejoice in successes, and sympathize with bad beats.

There's little doubt that without the television show *Celebrity Poker Showdown,* many of you probably would not have been inclined to pick up this book. I want to thank the producers, Andy Newman, Josh Malina, Bryan Scott, and Marcia Mule, for the opportunity to bring poker to a wide audience. I also thank my co-hosts Dave

Foley and Kevin Pollak for teaching me a little about TV and for listening to me talk about poker for hours and days on end. Lastly, I thank some of the celebrities whom I've had a chance to tutor, befriend, and spend some time with: Ben Affleck, Hank Azaria, Michael Ian Black, Tim Busfield, Don Cheadle, David Cross, Shannon Elizabeth, Peter Facinelli, Willie Garson, Jeff Gordon, Lauren Graham, Tom Green, Penn Jillette, Ron Livingston, Seth Meyers, Dave Navarro, Emily Procter, Mimi Rogers, Paul Rudd, David Schwimmer, Nicole Sullivan, Mena Suvari, and Travis Tritt. Special thanks to my friend Jon Favreau, who wrote and starred in one of my favorite movies of all time, *Swingers.* Jon is a huge fan of poker and I'm thrilled that he volunteered to write the introduction for this work.

And last but not least, there is no way I can ever sufficiently thank my co-author, Jonathan. We've worked very closely on this project, and I have tremendous respect for his intellect, his game, and his writing. With his tireless efforts and interviews, I believe we've created an excellent work that adds to the pantheon of poker literature. We'll be friends at and away from the table for a very long time. Thank you, Jonathan.

JONATHAN GROTENSTEIN

It all starts with the parents: Dad, who never tires of reminding me that his mother, a Brooklyn poker and pinochle sharp, always kept three hundred dollars pinned to the inside of her brassiere on the chance she'd encounter an action game; and Mom, who taught me canasta and backgammon when I was seven, then how to play for money when I was eight, ensuring my indebtedness to her not only emotionally, but in the more literal sense of the word. Thanks for supporting me through all of my adventures. I love you both very much.

Could Storms Reback have known what kind of mess he'd be getting us into when he sent me a photocopied article on the World Series of Poker, his handwritten notes scrawled all over the margins? The game has nourished us both beyond any reasonable expectations. Thank you, Storms, for being a friend, sounding board, and fellow traveler for almost half my life. (A debt of gratitude as well to the guy who wrote that article, Jim McManus—your lyrical take on the game was and continues to be an inspiration.)

Erick Brownstein and Bill Rotko believed I was a poker player long before I did. Judy Muller, defying every cliché you've ever heard about mothers-in-law, surprised me with her early support, thanks in part to her meeting a real-life success story in the form of Annie Duke. Nor would I have kept writing without unwavering encouragement from Erick, Bill, and Judy, friends like Laurie Arent, Jesse Wigutow, and Marsha Cooke, and the weekly dose of constructive criticism and relentlessly obscene banter that could only come from *Le Salón Anál.*

A lifetime's worth of thanks to Trish Boczkowski, who offered me a proposition rivaling anything Mr. Roarke gave to his guests on *Fantasy Island* when she asked if there was any chance that I'd be interested in writing a book, on poker, with one of the world's best players.

I couldn't have hoped for a better writing partner than Phil, who is an extremely funny, down-to-earth guy despite being over eleven feet tall. As a poker player, he is scary smart—I am still stinging from the ease with which he separated me from all of my sugar packets while teaching me "negotiation poker" over lunch at the Broadway Deli. Working together has made me a better writer and a much stronger poker player. Thank you, Phil.

Finally, to my wife, who doesn't always make it easy, but makes it all worthwhile. I love you, Kristen.

PHIL AND JONATHAN

Greg Dinkin and Frank Scatoni of Venture Literary are the best agents in the business. Their guidance and assistance in getting this book to your hands have been invaluable.

The folks at Simon Spotlight Entertainment are fantastic. Tricia Boczkowski has been the editor that writers dream of, maintaining our focus and always keeping us excited. Thanks also to Wendy Wagner, Russell Gordon, Julie Amitie, Nellie Kurtzman, Lynn Smith, Suzanne Murphy, Tracy van Straaten, Adam Rothberg, Jen Bergstrom, Robin Corey, Rick Richter, Emily Westlake, Bill Gaden, and Frank Fochetta, each invaluable in their assistance.

Finally, thanks to everyone else who contributed their time, effort, and expertise along the way: Lutz Bergman,

Andy Bloch, Joe Bob Briggs, T. J. Cloutier, Russell Daw, Antonio Esfandiari, Chris Ferguson, Layne Flack, Rafe Furst, Russ Hamilton, Jennifer Harman, Gary Horowitz, Andy Hughes, John Juanda, Todd Krieger, Howard Lederer, Mason Malmuth, Mike Matusow, Tex Morgan, Richard Sakai, Erik Seidel, and Sian Williams.

CONTENTS

FOREWORD

BY JON FAVREAU

The first time I saw poker on TV it was of as much interest to me as watching a koala bear size up a eucalyptus leaf. Whenever I flipped past the World Poker Tour it always seemed to be two bizarre-looking men staring interminably at each other and at a handful of cards scattered about the table. Nothing was happening, or so it seemed. Ducks look so peaceful as they sit on the pond, but under the surface their little webbed feet churn a mile a minute.

Somehow watching no-limit hold'em went from a laughable notion to a TiVo'd addiction. I don't know if it was the ridiculously colorful cast of characters or the spontaneous immediacy of the contest at hand. All I know is I was hooked. The more I watched, the more I wanted to watch.

One of the perks of being a member of the Hollywood community is that you get to actually enter your fantasies. I've gotten to dine with celebrities I've grown up idolizing

(I even host a TV show called *Dinner for Five* where I'm paid to do it), and I've gotten to actually *be* on TV shows that I had been a fan of. Being asked to compete in the WPT's *Hollywood Home Game* took it to another level completely. It was like a strange dream. You see, when you act on a TV show, you get to peer behind the curtain. Tony Soprano is really just an actor named Jimmy. Playing on the World Poker Tour is the equivalent of having a real sitdown with the real mobsters. I was really doing it. For real.

It was my first time playing no-limit. Sure, I'd played friendly games of seven-card stud and Omaha. I'd even tried a little low-stakes limit hold'em at a casino to bone up. But that's checkers, and no-limit is chess. I was actually on the WPT set playing the Cadillac of poker. I did pretty good for a rookie but ended up losing when all was said and done. I couldn't care less. I wanted to play again as soon as possible. The adrenaline kept me up for two nights just thinking about it.

I signed up for other Hollywood tournaments. I'm lucky enough to be able to freeroll into celebrity events. I got to cut my teeth for cheap. I even got to sit at tables and be in pots with the pros. It was at one of these events, in San Jose, where I met Phil Gordon. The first day of the tournament, world champions were being eliminated to my left and right. I was catching cards and had more than doubled my stack. Phil had been checking in with me during the breaks to give me advice. With this type of private coaching I was sure to shock the poker world and make the final table. He gave me a secret strategy that I knew in my heart would give me that extra edge I needed. I had my secret weapon. Within ten minutes of receiving my secret weapon I was knocked out and on my way to the airport. . . . *That's* how I met Phil Gordon. By the way, Phil won the tournament.

Poker has become a full-blown trend in Hollywood. It seems to be the bastard stepchild of the Cocktail Nation/Swingers thing. Somehow the Vegas aspect outlived the annoying cigar bar phase and is now settling into this weird no-limit hold'em gunfighter extravaganza. Every big star seems to want to buy in. It taps into both their competitive nature and proclivity for performance. Everyone, it seems, wants to be the fastest gun in the West. I can't tell you how many people in the business pop up at the casinos or host home games. And I don't mean the low-stakes pillow fights where your buy-in is the cover charge for a front row seat for an all-star funny fest. I'm talking about no-talking-if-you're-not-in-the-goddamn-pot-I'm-trying-to-think-here games.

This isn't to say it's not fun. All of the home tournaments I'm in cost about $20 to $25 to buy in. Nobody loses his shirt. The good thing about a serious game is that the stakes are irrelevant. My eardrums pound just as much when I go all-in if there's twenty on the line or two hundred thousand. It's about playing to win and playing to improve your game.

Phil Gordon has a laid-back and even approach to giving advice. He's also got the perspective of an insider, having lived the life long before it was a trend. There's also something to be said about a poker player who lives five minutes from the Bellagio and hasn't lost his ass. I invite you to enjoy and learn from this book.

INTRODUCTION

In July of 1991, just after my twenty-first birthday, I moved from a small suburb of Atlanta, Georgia, out to Santa Cruz, California, for an engineering job with a small software development firm. My first day at the company's "halfway house," a place where they put up all their new recruits, I met a guy who would become a lifelong friend.

Jay was from Chicago, and, unlike me, he had many friends living in the Bay area. Just a week later, one of Jay's friends took him to a place in San Jose, just a thirty-five-minute drive from our apartment, called "Garden City."

"Phil, you will not believe what I saw tonight," he told me when he got home. "Poker is *legal* in California! There is this place in San Jose where there are like two hundred people playing real poker for real money. They're playing a game called Texas Hold'em or something like that."

I had played poker, and won, as a kid with my great-aunt and parents. I had played poker, and won, at summer camps throughout high school. I had played poker, and won, with the guys in college. It was 10:30 P.M. on a

Tuesday night. I had $63 on me, another $1,300 in my brand-new checking account, and a $1,000 signing bonus check that was just about to clear.

Impetuous youths that we were, we decided to go and check it out. I had to see for myself. I was very nervous in the car, decidedly apprehensive that we were going to an underground, illegal game where guys would be cheating our asses off and someone was likely to get hurt. Jay assured me that his buddy had actually played in the game and that it was completely legal and square.

We arrived at the sprawling parking lot at about 11:45 P.M. A burly security guard asked us for ID at the door. Spread before us were about fifty tables, most completely full, guys in white tuxedo shirts and black ties at each table deftly handling cards, scantily clad waitresses serving cocktails, and patrons tossing chips into massive pots. It didn't seem possible.

We asked a waitress to point us to the guy in charge. We met the floorman and started asking questions: "This is completely legal?" Yes. "The chips are real? For real money?" Yes. "What game do they play?" Texas Hold'em. "How do you play?"

The guy laughed. "Here boys, take a look at this." He handed us a brochure on the rules of Texas Hold'em, and told us to tell him when we would like to join a game in progress—two seats were open in the $1/2 limit hold'em game, $40 **buy-in.***

We devoured the brochure, completely enthralled, and watched from the rail for about an hour discussing all the

---

* Words that appear in bold at their first appearance in the text are poker terms whose definitions can be found in the glossary at the end of this book.

fine points of strategy: the white "dealer" button, the blinds, check-raise (can that really be legal?), all-in (why exactly don't they let them take money out of their pockets?), the fact that a pair of aces "in the hole" seemed like the best hand, but it seemed like just about any two cards down could win. We were ready.

At 1:00 A.M. on a Wednesday morning in San Jose, California, I became a poker player.

At 1:45 A.M., I became a poker player on the way to the ATM machine for a $40 withdrawal and a rebuy.

We left at 6 A.M., both completely broke. We called in sick the next day and spent most of the afternoon talking strategy, analyzing the play from the previous night, and playing practice hands face up on the living room floor. Our startling conclusion: any two cards really can win! At 4 P.M. we left the apartment, stopped by the bank to pick up some cash—our ATM withdrawal limit had already been maxed out—and returned to Garden City.

Ten years and a hundred thousand hands later, I found myself in Las Vegas at the Final Table of the $10,000 buy-in 2001 World Series of Poker championship event. There were five players left: Phil Hellmuth Jr., Carlos Mortensen, Dewey Tomko, Stan Schrier, and me. Four million of the $6,000,000 prize pool was left to be claimed, $1,500,000 for first, along with the title and the coveted gold bracelet.

I came in fourth, earning $400,000, and realized I had covered a lot of ground since those experiences at the $1-$2 table. I read nearly every poker book written. I played in casinos across the globe. I talked with and befriended the best players in the world. I studied the game.

The players on the World Poker Tour make it seem so

easy—a $1,000,000 bluff here, a great read and call there, a late position steal from the short stack, a well-timed re-raise with a second pair. But for the new player, like me in 1991, poker is intimidating. This book, I hope, should help.

There are tons of strategy books out there, some good, some not so good. They offer advice like: "If you have ace-queen **offsuit** in middle position, raise if you're the first in the pot, or call up to a single raise." This is *not* that book.

This is a book about the poker lifestyle.

What's the poker lifestyle, you ask? It's everything I learned from July 1991 to May 2001: how the game works, the books worth reading, what to expect at a cardroom, playing online, moving from low-limit to middle-limit to high-limit, entering and winning tournaments, and how to know you're ready to turn pro.

Texas Hold'em is not an easy game. Nobody goes from home game chump to World Poker Tour champ overnight. With some hard work, study, and discipline, you can be a winning player. You've taken the right first step, buying this book. Now, take a seat at the table and come along for a wild, fun ride.

1

A BRIEF HISTORY OF POKER

*Play is older than culture, for culture, however inadequately
defined, always presupposes human society, and animals
have not waited for man to teach them their playing.*
—JOHAN HUIZINGA, *Homo Ludens*

What is the greatest human achievement of all time? Some might argue for the discovery of fire. Organized religion. Space travel. The *Sports Illustrated* swimsuit issue.

But what about the discovery of play?

Think about it: Before play, people had to satisfy their competitive urges by beating each other over the head with big sticks. In today's society, playing is so ingrained that we take it for granted. How much time, money, and

energy do we dedicate to watching, betting on, and otherwise living and dying by college and professional sports?
What is the entertainment industry if not the evolution of
ancient play? Businessmen play the stock market.
Politicians play to their audiences. Bachelors and bache-
lorettes looking for love (or something less high-minded)
play the field.

Who knows what the first "games" were? "Hey, Wulfgar,
my stack of hides is larger than yours." "Yeah? Well, I can
throw this rock farther than you can."

Whatever these games were like, they made a quantum
leap when somebody discovered playing cards.

One thousand years after the discovery of paper, a feat
most historians attribute to the Chinese around 100 B.C.E.,
the Emperor Mu-Tsung celebrated New Year's Eve playing
a game of "paper dominoes" with his wife. We don't know
who won that contest, but if the empress played anything
like Jennifer Harman or Annie Duke, the emperor may
have lost his silk shirt.

This new fad made its way to the Islamic world, where
"cups" and "swords" were added to the traditional
Chinese "circles" and "bamboos" to create the first four-
suited deck of cards. Some innovative Muslims began
including "court cards" as well, representing the *malik*
(king), *na'ib malik* (vice-king), and *thani na'ib* (vice-vice-
king).

No one is exactly sure when these decks swept into
Europe. What we do know is that in 1377, a Swiss monk
found card playing fascinating enough to put quill to
paper and produced a manuscript on the subject of card
games. He wasn't alone—fast-forward only twenty years,

and the powers-that-were in France, Germany, and Italy have already begun regulating the time, place, and amounts wagered by their card-crazed subjects. It was, perhaps, a great time for finding loose games.

We have to thank the French for our modern-day cards. They not only re-jiggered the deck to align with their own notions of royalty—kings, queens, and jacks replaced the Muslim court cards—but they also replaced the four suits with their current-day counterparts. An early French deck featured Charlemagne as the king of diamonds, Emperor Julius Caesar as the king of hearts, Alexander the Great as the king of clubs, and biblical King David as the king of spades.

VIVE LA DIFFÉRENCE!

The "American" fifty-two-card deck, which was actually designed by the French, might be regarded by most as the world's standard, but it's certainly not the world's only deck.

To this day, traditional German decks consist of only thirty-two cards, bearing leaves, acorns, and bells instead of spades, diamonds, and clubs. Their court cards have a more military bent—no queens and jacks, but the all-male Obers ("over-officers") and Unters ("under-officers").

Spain's forty-card deck—kings, knights, valets, and the numbers one through seven—are divided into swords, cups, coins, and real clubs, i.e., heavy sticks you might hit somebody over the head with after receiving a **bad beat**.

The Swiss and Italians also have their own variations.

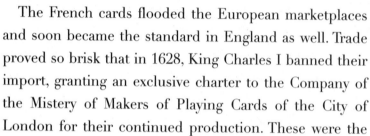

The French cards flooded the European marketplaces and soon became the standard in England as well. Trade proved so brisk that in 1628, King Charles I banned their import, granting an exclusive charter to the Company of the Mistery of Makers of Playing Cards of the City of London for their continued production. These were the first decks to cross the Atlantic, as the British monarchy forbade its colonists from manufacturing any of their own. The upstart Americans, bristling from the exorbitant excise taxes they were forced to pay on their playing cards (and a few other goods as well) decided to revolt.

Free from the yoke of British rule, the new Yankee ingenuity soon made its mark on the history of playing cards. American manufacturers introduced double-headed court cards (no more having to read the card upside down), varnished surfaces (more durable, easier to shuffle), and rounded corners (less wear and tear). These decks, like the rest of the new country, began moving west.

THE CHEATER'S GAME

*The frontier gambler of history was not always tall and thin;
he was often short and sometimes quite stout. His hair was
frequently fair rather than dark, and sometimes he wore a
full beard. There were some gamblers who neglected to shave
and still others were beardless because they were women.
Some of the professional gamblers of the western frontier
were scrupulously honest and some were as crooked as a
Colorado creek bed. There were the generous and the nig-
gardly, the courageous and the cowardly, the intelligent and
the stupid. They were, in a word, human, with all the virtues
and vices of any other segment of mankind.*
—ROBERT K. DEARMENT, *Knights of the Green Cloth*

In 1834, American writer Jonathan H. Green noticed a
new game growing in popularity among the gamblers who
rode the riverboats up and down the Mississippi. It
involved only twenty cards (tens through aces), a fair
degree of bluffing, and an enormous amount of cheating.
So much, in fact, that Green—who would go on to write a
tell-all about the troubles he'd seen called *The Exposures
of the Arts and the Miseries of Gambling*—described it as
"the Cheating Game." The gentlemen (and ladies) who
played it, however, called it something else.

Some etymologists argue that "poker" derives from
hocus pocus, a popular expression among magicians of the
day. Others believe that it came from *poke,* a slang word
used by criminals to describe pickpocketing. There were
some similarities to the French card game *poque* (which
we vulgar Americans would have pronounced "pokah"),
and even more to the German *Pochspiel,* a bluffing game
where players opened a round of betting by declaring *Ich
Poche!* Both of these games may have been derived from a

Persian game called *As-Naz,* which translates to something akin to "my beloved ace." But as some historians
point out, there were no aces in the original Persian
decks, meaning they must have learned the game from
someone else. Like so many things American, the game
seems to be a mishmash of elements begged, borrowed,
and stolen from other cultures.

These early games along the Mississippi gave birth to
an entirely new, uniquely American character: the riverboat gambler. Their stories are the stuff of legend. Like
J. J. Bryant, a Virginian who ran away from home to join
the circus (where he swallowed swords and walked the
"slack-wire"), dabbling in slave trade and hotel management before finding his niche as a poker player. Or
Charles Cora, an Italian cardsharp raised from infancy by
the Louisiana madam of a bordello in Natchez-Under-the-
Hill, a town described by many at the time as the most
lawless place in America.

As pioneers pushed west, establishing towns and settle-
ments wherever there was something to farm or mine,
poker moved with them. The latter half of the nineteenth
century was a heyday for frontier gamblers who engaged in
high-stakes poker games designed to separate these set-
tlers from their herds and lucky strikes. These games occasionally resolved with violence (quite literally resulting in
the poker expression **under the gun**), and often led to
financial ruin, as in the case of former Kansas governor
Thomas Carney, who in 1877 lost everything he had in one
legendary hand to Dodge City poker pro "Colonel" Charlie
Norton. Carney pushed **all-in** with four kings, but Norton
had him covered with four aces. Carney never recovered.

Along the way, the deck was expanded to include fifty-two cards. Open cards became popular during the Civil War, giving rise to stud poker. Antes and wildcards were introduced in the 1870s, lowball and split pot games sometime around 1900.

At the turn of the last century, however, the general tenor of the Old West was changing into something more family-friendly. New laws were enacted to banish gambling—and poker along with it—from most of the states where it had flourished.

Well, not everywhere. In progressive California, the attorney general possessed the infinite wisdom to declare poker not a game of chance, but a game of skill, laying the groundwork for the still-vibrant cardroom culture that exists there today.* Nevada followed suit in the 1930s. And "road games" thrived in the back rooms of bars and pool halls, where great fortunes continued to be won and lost.

MEANWHILE, DEEP IN THE HEART OF TEXAS . . .

Mr. Moss, I have to let you go.
— NICK "THE GREEK" DANDALOS

According to a survey taken by the U.S. Playing Card Company in 1946, contract bridge was far and away the country's favorite game. Newspapers ran front page stories dedicated to its champions—names like Ely Culbertson,

---

* While these are the "facts" presented by most poker authorities, this may be an apocryphal story, if not downright untrue. The actual statute prohibiting gambling in California was passed in 1872. In the 1940s, when the state tried to shut down Ernie Primm's Embassy Club in Gardena, it was discovered that those nineteenth-century legislators had somehow overlooked the inclusion of poker in the statute, presumably for the sake of their own regular games.

Helen Sobel, even a team called "Four Aces." Yes, bridge was huge. Poker ran second among men, about as popular as pinochle, and generated even less interest among women.

Things were different in Texas, however, where poker-playing cowboys and rustlers regularly mixed it up in high-stakes contests, often forced to move from place to place to stay ahead of the law. The games retained a good deal of the character of the Old West. That is to say, they were often marred by violence and cheating, but in the end proved to be just as mythic in stature.

When Lester Ben "Benny" Binion was finally forced to leave Dallas in 1939, after evading conviction on charges that included bootlegging, theft, possession of a concealed weapon, and two counts of murder, he was considered one of the kings of the Texas gambling scene. He wound up in the only city where his vices were virtues—Las Vegas—where he purchased the downtown Horseshoe Casino. It wasn't as glamorous as the places on the Strip, but under Binion's management, it soon developed a reputation as a place that would take any bet, any size, any time.

In 1949, Nick "the Greek" Dandalos agreed to let Binion host what was at the time the highest-stakes no-limit poker game in history. Dandalos, a refined, well-schooled gentleman of fifty-seven, was a legend on the East Coast, where he had reportedly broken every house that would take his action to the tune of some sixty million dollars. He had never, however, faced Johnny Moss, considered by many to be the best poker player in Texas, which, by extension, meant the world. Binion knew this reputation to be well founded, having bankrolled Moss from time to time back in Dallas, and Moss, as this fable goes, although exhausted from a four-day poker marathon, boarded the first plane to Las Vegas upon receiving Binion's call.

Moss and Dandalos battled heads up for the next five months in an epic contest that covered the poker spectrum: five-card stud, draw, seven-card stud, seven-card high-low split, lowball, both ace-to-the-five and deuce-to-the-seven. Dandalos nearly broke Moss after delivering one of the most memorable bad beats in the recorded history of the game (the details of which are omitted here, as no one likes a **bad beat story**). The wily Texan recovered, however, and methodically pounded the Greek into submission. The game finally ended when, after having lost a rumored four million dollars, Dandalos rose from the table and announced famously, "Mr. Moss, I have to let you go."

It was a publicity stunt that succeeded beyond Binion's expectations. Twenty-one years later, he decided to repeat it and invited a handful of the world's best poker players to compete in a promotional tournament he dubbed the "World Series of Poker."

THE GAME IS TEXAS HOLD'EM

Texas Hold'em is an extremely complicated form of poker. This is because the exact manner in which a hand should be played is often debatable. It is not uncommon to hear two expert players argue the pros and cons of a certain strategy.
— DAVID SKLANSKY AND MASON MALMUTH,
Hold'em Poker for Advanced Players

When the California courts finally conceded that poker was a legal game of skill, they were talking about draw poker. Five cards dealt to each player. A round of betting, then a draw, giving each player the chance to replace some of the cards in his or her hand with new ones.

Their ruling, however, did not extend to stud poker, that class of games that incorporates face-up cards in some way or another. Stud remained, in the eyes of California state legislators, an illegal game of chance until 1987.

As with so many legal distinctions, this one was more than a little bit ironic. While draw poker has its fair share of subtle strategies and complexities, it doesn't give an expert player anywhere near the advantage that a stud game will. The ability to see cards, represent a hand, make a read on an opponent's hand—these are qualities that are, for many players, the most artful and skillful aspects of the game.

Draw might also be an easier game to cheat at, which is probably one of the reasons it remained the most popular form of poker for so many years. But if you were to sit down with a group of players in the 1940s or '50s, odds were they'd be dealing stud. Draw may have been the game of hustlers and riverboat gamblers, but stud games were the pastime of the United States Armed Services. Harry S. Truman, who probably learned poker during his stint in the First World War, was an avid fan of five-card stud before, during, and after his presidency. According to Bruce Lambert, a regular in his weekly game, Truman was a chump: "He wanted to see what your hole card was, and knew anyone got a kick out of winning from him and he accommodated . . . but if he could whip you he got a big kick out of it."

Richard "Tricky Dick" Nixon played a somewhat shrewder game during his time in the Navy in World War II. A fellow officer estimated that Nixon milked some $6,000 or $7,000 out of his shipmates during his tour of duty, which, according to rumor, he snuck home in a secret compartment at the bottom of his footlocker and used to finance his first run for Congress.

As conscription required nearly every American male to serve, stud poker enjoyed several decades as the country's most popular game. Sometime during the 1960s, however, a variant of the game began to sneak into wider circulation. A. D. Livingston, a semi-professional poker player and author who has written on everything from poker strategy to cooking shellfish, described his first experience in an article for *Life* magazine:

> They called the game Hold Me Darling, or Hold Me for short. Each player received two cards face down. A round of betting followed. Then three communal cards were turned up in the middle. Another bet. Another turn card. Another bet. Final turn card. Final bet. Showdown. Simple enough? Well, yes, mechanically. But strategically and mathematically it was different from any poker game I had ever run up against.

Livingston couldn't find reference to "Hold Me Darling" in any of his books on poker. He called a player he knew in Colorado to ask him if he'd ever run into the game. "Never heard of it . . . but a new game has really caught on. High Hold'em. Each player gets two down cards. You bet on 'em. Then three cards are turned up in the middle . . ."

In his 1967 book *The Complete Guide to Winning Poker*, Albert Morehead mourns the passing of an era: "Thirty years ago, two-thirds of the professional games were five-card stud; today, not one-tenth are."

Some of that action went to the California games, where lowball draw was hugely popular in the 1960s and '70s, or to tables featuring other new variants like "Omaha" and "Amarillo."* Felton "Corky" McCorquodale, a Texan transplanted to Las Vegas, introduced Hold Me—which he, like everyone else in his home state, called "Texas Hold'em"—to the poker room at the Golden Nugget in the early 1960s. The game's popularity grew quickly among the poker-savvy, as its structure allowed a good player to risk a relatively small amount to win much more. A few years later, Texas Hold'em was chosen to be the featured game at the first World Series of Poker.

In what should come as no surprise, Texans utterly dominated the early years of the World Series. Johnny Moss won the first two, in 1970 and 1971, and again in 1974. "Amarillo Slim" Preston, a full-blooded Texan save for the technicality of having been born in Arkansas, won in 1972. Brian "Sailor" Roberts of San Angelo earned the crown in 1975, Doyle "Texas Dolly" Brunson of Longsworth owned the following two.

Shortly after winning his second bracelet, Texas Dolly was overcome by a mad idea: to write the best book of all time on the game he excelled at. The resulting work did for poker what Prometheus did for fire.

---

* "Amarillo" is actually the game we call "Omaha" today, requiring a player to use two and exactly two of their four hole cards. What used to be called "Omaha" is today sometimes referred to as "Tulsa." In any case, it's easy to see why the game of poker owes so much to Texas and its immediate neighbors.

THE '80S

But now that they've read the book, they recognize what I'm doing, they think I'm bluffing, and call me. It's hampered my style. I used to be able to wreck a game without holding any cards at all, because I never got called. Now I need the cards.
— DOYLE BRUNSON, ON WRITING *Super/System*

Texas Dolly Brunson wasn't always destined to be a poker player. He was a hell of a basketball player, once considered to be one of the ten best college players in the country, before a severely broken leg ended his dreams of going pro.

A basketball player can't win a game on his or her own. Brunson understood this, of course, so in setting out to write the best poker book of all time, he gathered five players whom he considered to be the best and brightest minds on the subject.

Armed with a tape recorder, Brunson talked to each of them about their specialty. "Crazy Mike" Caro on draw poker. David "Chip" Reese on seven-card stud. Joey "Howard Hughes" Hawthorne on lowball. David "Einstein" Sklansky on high-low. Bobby "The Owl" Baldwin on limit hold'em. And Texas Dolly himself would pen a chapter on no-limit hold'em, a game that he described as "the Cadillac of poker games."

The book was originally called *How I Made Over $1,000,000 Playing Poker,* but Brunson, who published it out of pocket, changed the title to *Super/System: A Course in Power Poker* in the hopes of improving its initially weak sales. It contained a glossary of poker terms that would go on to capture the imaginations of millions of new players:

Bad beats. **Crying calls**. The **turn**. The **river**. The **nuts**. Brunson also included almost fifty pages of statistical charts, revealing to the world-at-large secrets like the chances of hitting a **gut-shot** straight with three cards to come in seven-card stud (about 23 percent), or the odds of being dealt a five-card full house (693-to-1).

Super/System and the books that would follow forever democratized the game of poker. A beginner could read the book, study the charts, and know more than many life-long players. A healthy knowledge of mathematics could substitute for years of hard-knock experience.

Suddenly, the Texas backroom players found themselves sharing the winner's circle with kids who had learned to play in their college dormitories, or grinders from underground card clubs in New York City. The World Series began to attract a steady flow of international players. The payouts got bigger. And the game got a little flashier.

Witness Stu Ungar. Photographic memory and a genius IQ. He dropped out of school at fifteen to become a professional gin rummy player. The Kid, as he came to be known, destroyed games up and down the East Coast, destroying himself in the process with heavy drug use and heavier sports betting. By the time he got to Las Vegas in 1976, the twenty-three-year-old was dead broke. Ungar somehow scraped together the buy-in for a $50,000 gin tournament. He won, of course, but couldn't resist forecasting each of his opponent's cards on the final two hands in front of a crowd full of gaping onlookers. A scary feat, enough to frighten anyone from playing gin rummy with the Kid, or at least not for any serious money. It would end his gin rummy career.

He moved on to blackjack. One night at Caesar's Palace, after Ungar had won $83,000, a casino manager barred him from further play. Ungar retaliated by correctly naming the last eighteen cards in the single-deck blackjack shoe. He was reportedly blacklisted thereafter by nearly every casino.

Ever in search of action, Ungar entered the 1980 World Series of Poker having had virtually no experience playing no-limit hold'em. He won. He won again the next year. After disappearing for most of the '90s—presumably lost to his two addictions, drugs and gambling—he returned in 1997, when, backed by a mysterious benefactor, he entered again . . . and won. During the course of his life, Ungar played around thirty no-limit hold'em championship events, winning an incredible ten of them!*

Ungar blazed a trail for a new breed of players who didn't raise with a Southern twang. In 1987, Hong Kong native Johnny Chan crossed the Pacific to take the first of two consecutive titles; Englishman Mansour Matloubi broke the Atlantic barrier when he won in 1990. Poker was no longer the cherished possession of Texas, or even, for that matter, America.

MIKE McDERMOTT

Why do you think the same five guys are at the finals of the World Series of Poker EVERY year? They're the luckiest guys in Vegas?
— MATT DAMON AS MIKE McDERMOTT, *Rounders*

---

* Two months after taking down the one-million-dollar prize, he was broke again. A little over a year later, in the midst of a cocaine, methadone, and Percodan binge, Ungar's heart simply gave out.

In 1998, the same year that Scottie Nguyen took the gold bracelet and began a legacy of great Vietnamese poker players (several of whom share his last name), Miramax Films released a modestly budgeted movie called *Rounders*. Matt Damon, on the heels of all kinds of acclaim for *Good Will Hunting*, played Mike McDermott, a young, aggressive poker player who steamrolls over college fraternity games, takes it to the tourists, and finally faces down Teddy KGB (John Malkovich), a crafty Russian with a weakness for Oreo cookies.

It wasn't the first great poker movie (an honor that probably belongs to *The Cincinnati Kid*), but it was a relative financial success for Miramax, grossing around twenty-two million dollars domestically. That's a small fraction of what it was worth to the poker world.

"Mike McDermott," a Hollywood Park Casino regular once observed, "was responsible for a lot of dumb money."

Hordes of young players began picking up the game. Most of them were, in the parlance of poker, **donors**. They contributed something else, however, that proved to be far more important than their loose money: They gave the game cultural currency. Poker players didn't have to be Texas cowboys or Vegas gruffs with pinkie rings and cigars. They could be like, well, Matt Damon.

There's a scene in *Rounders* where Mike and his ex-girlfriend watch a video, Johnny Chan trapping Erik Seidel's pair of queens with the nut straight to win the 1988 World Series. It's compelling stuff.

The scene spurred a demand to see other compelling stuff. Poker had been on TV since the early 1990s, mostly edited highlight reels of the World Series. But while it can be ridiculously exciting to play poker, it's not the most exciting game to watch. Let's face it, turning over two cards to reveal a set of nines doesn't pack anywhere near the wallop of a diving touchdown catch or fastbreak alley-oop. Poker is a game of the mind, and there's no way to televise what goes on in someone's mind, not in real-time, anyway.

That is, until 1999, when British Channel 4 UK broadcast the first episode of *Late Night Poker,* a decently staked game by today's standards featuring memorable characters like "Barmy" Barney Boatman, Dave "Devilfish" Ulliott, Joe "The Elegance" Beevers, and "Crazy Horse" Ram Vaswani. More unique than the players was the table itself: It was made of glass, allowing television cameras underneath the table to film a player's hole cards. Every successful bluff and every carefully laid trap was like an inside joke shared between you and the winner. A miraculous river card let you experience, at the same time, the ecstasy of incredible luck and the agony of the insufferable bad beat.

Across the pond, Americans were experimenting with tables equipped with tiny "lipstick" cameras, allowing TV viewers and commentators to see the hole cards in the same instant as the player. Sixteen of these cameras were used, in concert with ten microphones, to give a tournament called the Five Diamond Classic the most extensive coverage that had ever been afforded a poker game. And so the World Poker Tour was born. As was poker's first TV star, the show's winner, previously unknown Gus Hansen, an aggressive young Mike McDermott type—from Denmark.

♥ ♦ ♣ ♠ ♥ ♦ ♣ ♠ ♥ ♦ ♣ ♠ ♥ ♦ ♣ ♠ ♥ ♦ ♣ ♠ ♥ ♦ ♣ ♠ ♥ ♦ ♣ ♠

YOUR DEFINING MOMENT

When a Defining Moment comes along, you define the
moment . . . or the moment defines you.
— KEVIN COSTNER AS ROY MCAVOY, *Tin Cup*

Okay, it's a quote from a golf movie. But the same sentiment
applies to poker. As a player, you'll repeatedly be faced with
critical decisions that will forever alter an outcome, whether
of a hand, a tournament, or your poker career.

Your first Defining Moment, however, won't be anything so intense. Demonstrate your knowledge of popular
poker lore by matching the poker quote to the movie. If
for some reason you haven't seen one of these movies, get
down to the video store and do your homework.

1. *My Little Chickadee* (1940). W. C. Fields is Cuthbert J.
   Twillie, a poker-playing con man whose life gets
   interrupted by Mae West.

2. *The Cincinnati Kid* (1965). Up-and-comer Steve McQueen
   looks to prove himself against old pro Edward G.
   Robinson. Lays the groundwork for all of the poker
   archetypes and offers the greatest bad beat in the history
   of poker cinema.

3. *A Big Hand for the Little Lady* (1966). When her husband
   (Henry Fonda) loses the family savings in a poker game—
   then suffers a heart attack—it's up to Joanne Woodward
   to win it back. First, however, she's got to learn how to
   play poker.

4. *Cool Hand Luke* (1967). Paul Newman is a free spirit who
   can't be broken by prison, beatings, or eating fifty eggs in
   an hour. It's his bluffing prowess at the poker table,
   however, that earns him his nickname.

5. *California Split* (1974). George Segal and Elliot Gould are L.A. gamblers trying to figure out if they're in it for the action or the score. Directed by Robert Altman, with a cameo by one Amarillo Slim Preston as, of course, himself.

6. *The House of Games* (1987). David Mamet's twisty thriller about a female psychiatrist who gets mixed up with a professional con artist includes a great scene at the poker table.

7. *Havana* (1990). Robert Redford plays Jack Weil, a 1950s professional poker player who heads to Havana to set up a game, only to fall in love and get mixed up in the whole Cuban Revolution thing.

8. *Rounders* (1998). Matt Damon is a gambler trying to reform his ways, Ed Norton is his old friend who is trying to stop him. It leads to a classic confrontation between Damon and John Malkovich, hamming it up as Russian poker sharp Teddy KGB.

_____ a. "You know what cheers me up when I'm feeling shitty? Rolled-up aces over kings. Check-raising stupid tourists and taking huge pots off of them. Stacks and towers of checks I can't even see over. Playing all-night high-limit hold'em at the Taj, 'where the sand turns to gold.'"

_____ b. "You can't bluff someone who's not paying attention."

_____ c. "If a thing is worth having, it's worth cheating for."

_____ d. "Gets down to what it's all about, doesn't it? Making the wrong move at the right time."

_____ e. "I try to keep the gambling to a minimum." "How do you do that?" "By being good at it."

_____ f. "I wouldn't play poker with Henry Drummond if his back was to a mirror! Even if I had the money!"

_____ g. "Old Blue out of chute number two!"

_____ h. "Yeah, well, sometimes nothin' can be a real cool hand."

♥ ♦ ♣ ♠ ♥ ♦ ♣ ♠ ♥ ♦ ♣ ♠ ♥ ♦ ♣ ♠ ♥ ♦ ♣ ♠ ♥ ♦ ♣ ♠ ♥ ♦ ♣ ♠

THE ANSWERS

1 **c** "If a thing is worth having, it's worth cheating for."
    —My Little Chickadee

2 **d** "Gets down to what it's all about, doesn't it? Making the
    wrong move at the right time."*—The Cincinnati Kid*

3 **f** "I wouldn't play poker with Henry Drummond if his back
    was to a mirror! Even if I had the money!"
    —A Big Hand for the Little Lady

4 **h** "Yeah, well, sometimes nothin' can be a real cool hand."
    —Cool Hand Luke

5 **g** "Old Blue out of chute number two!"*—California Split*

6 **b** "You can't bluff someone who's not paying attention."
    —The House of Games

7 **e** "I try to keep the gambling to a minimum."
    "How do you do that?"
    "By being good at it."*—Havana*

8 **a** "You know what cheers me up when I'm feeling shitty?
    Rolled-up aces over kings. Check-raising stupid tourists
    and taking huge pots off of them. Stacks and towers of
    checks I can't even see over. Playing all-night high-limit
    hold'em at the Taj, 'where the sand turns to gold.'"
    —Rounders

2

THE BASICS

Poker became the national card game of the United States because it so well suits the American temperament. It is a game for the individual. Each player is on his own, the master of his fate. . . . It fits any situation, whether it is a serious game among experts or a hilarious game for the entertainment of family and friends who just want to have a good time. . . . Poker is easy to learn, and once learned is never forgotten. And the cost of the equipment is inconsiderable; there is no more economical form of recreation than card-playing.

—ALBERT H. MOREHEAD,
The Complete Guide to Winning Poker

Y ou've immersed yourself in the history of poker, maybe you've rented some of the movies. You don't know it yet, but you've developed an itch that only poker can scratch. As the old joke goes, "Sex is good, but poker lasts longer."

THE CARDS

Obviously, the first thing you'll need to embark on your poker career is a deck of cards. Many professional poker players carry one with them at all times. They're especially useful on airplanes or in restaurants, where you'll always be able to deal a hand of "negotiation poker" or "Lenny's Delight" . . . but we'll get to that later.

While you can play with any fifty-two-card deck, a stickler for details will tell you that standard poker cards are $3\frac{1}{2}$" x $2\frac{1}{2}$". Fortunately, unless you grew up in a house with a bridge *parlor*, poker cards are what you have always considered to be a normal deck. (The deck used for bridge, a game where you have to hold a lot of cards at once, is a little narrower.)

The first choice is one that you've probably had to make before: paper or plastic.

Paper cards are relatively inexpensive, but they start to deteriorate after a few sessions. Bee and Bicycle are the most common brands used by casinos and cardrooms, but if you do some digging, you'll discover all kinds of interesting alternatives, like Mohawks, Steamboats, and Torpedoes.

Plastic cards, which are used in many casinos, are a lot more durable, a little bit easier to shuffle, and they can even be washed with soap and water. They're also about five times more expensive than paper cards, but the companies that make them (Kem and Royal, to name two) promise that they'll last long enough to pay for themselves many times over.

If you're looking to depart from the classic tradition,

there are plenty of manufacturers and novelty shops that will let you design your own cards, from a simple monogram on the back to the faces of your family members on the front.

THE DONDORF DECK

Today's playing cards are mass-produced in fairly generic styles, but it hasn't always been this way. One notable exception was the Dondorf Company, a German family of artisans who, from 1833 to 1933, unveiled series after series of unique designs that many collectors claim were the most beautiful cards ever produced.

To celebrate the company's 100th anniversary, the Dondorfs designed what would be their most lavish and intricate deck to date, produced in the most limited of limited editions and handed out at the centennial festivities. The elaborate design on the backs of the cards demanded sixteen separate color printings; the intricately detailed fronts required twelve more of their own.

The anniversary deck proved to be the end of the Dondorfs. The cost of printing the cards, coupled with the economic depression that had swept the world, drove the proud company into bankruptcy.

While idealism may have killed the artist, the

legacy lives on today: Altenburger-Stralsunder, the company that purchased the remains of the Dondorf operation, continues to make reproductions of many Dondorf designs.

THE LANGUAGE OF BETTING

Before you can start playing, you have to learn the language of betting. Fortunately, there aren't that many words. Every time the action gets to you, you're going to have to do one of five things:

1. **Fold**. Lay your hand down and exit the pot.
2. **Call**. Match the bet that is in front of you. If there is no bet in front of you, you can . . .
3. **Check** (pass or "no bet," if you're British) the action to the next player,
4. **Bet** (if you're the first person to act), or
5. **Raise** someone else's bet.

Knowing those five words will allow you to communicate with poker players all over the world. Feel the power coursing through your veins.

THE DEAL

For those new to Texas Hold'em, it is probably the easiest form of widow poker to learn, "widow" being a somewhat more colorful term for cards dealt in the center of the table that are shared by each of the players. In hold'em, these community cards—five in all—are called the **board.**

Almost every hold'em game played today incorporates what's called a **blind.** Some use a single blind—a mandatory bet posted by the player just to the left of the dealer—but most incorporate a **big blind** (whatever the table rules determine to be a full bet) and a **small blind** (a fraction of that full bet).

Blinds, like their cousin the **ante**, are designed to encourage action. Think about it this way: Without blinds, the first person to throw in a bet would be risking money to win nothing. These aren't appealing odds to a thinking poker player, who wouldn't open the betting without the strongest of hands. The blinds, however, create instant **pot odds** (a concept we'll get into later), giving a player the chance to win something more than what he or she has wagered.

Once the blinds have been posted, play proceeds as follows:

1. Two cards—the **hole cards**—are dealt facedown to each player.
2. The player sitting to the left of the big blind—the position known as under the gun—has the option to call or raise the blind. Betting continues around the table. You have to pay to play: If you don't call a bet (or any subsequent raises), you have to fold.

3. Once the round of betting has been completed, a group of three cards—better known as the **flop**—is laid faceup on the table.

4. Another round of betting is initiated by the player sitting closest to the left of the dealer (often the small blind). Unlike the opening round, you don't have to bet—you can opt to check instead. If someone else bets, however, you're going to have to call or raise to stay in.

5. Another community card, also known as **fourth street** or the **turn**, is dealt, followed by another round of betting, once again initiated by the person sitting closest to the dealer's left who still happens to be in the pot.

6. A final community card, **fifth street** or the **river**, is placed on the table. A final round of betting ensues.

7. Showdown. The best hand wins.

8. The deal moves to the left and the cycle repeats.

SHOWDOWNS

If you're reading this book, you probably already know all about showdowns. In the unlikely event that you don't, or you just don't remember whether a straight flush beats a full house, you may want to commit the following to memory:

Royal Flush
A straight, ace to ten, all of the same suit.

    Ex. | A♥ | K♥ | Q♥ | J♥ | 10♥ |

Straight Flush

Any five consecutive cards of the same suit.

Ex. 2♣ 3♣ 4♣ 5♣ 6♣

Four of a Kind

Exactly what you'd think it would be. Also called a **case**.

Ex. K♠ K♣ K♥ K♦ 4♦

Full House

Three of a kind, plus two of a kind. This hand would be "fours full of threes." Also called a **boat**.

Ex. 4♦ 4♥ 4♣ 3♦ 3♠

Flush

Any five cards of the same suit. The hand below is a queen-high flush, which would lose to a king-high flush, etc. If the highest card is a community card, ties get broken by the second card, third card, etc.

Ex. Q♥ 10♥ 7♥ 4♥ 2♥

Straight

Five consecutive cards of any suit.

Ex. 10♣ 9♥ 8♣ 7♦ 6♦

Three of a Kind

Also called **trips** or a **set**.

Ex. 6♣ 6♥ 6♦ A♠ 8♦

Two Pair

The example below would be "queens and jacks"
or "queens over jacks."

Ex. [Q♥] [Q♦] [J♥] [J♣] [3♥]

One Pair

If your two matching cards are both hidden, you
have a **pocket pair**.

Ex. [A♠] . [A♥]   [K♥] [9♦♦] [4♣♣]

High Cards

If no one has a hand, the highest card (or cards)
win(s).

Ex. [A♠] . [9♦♦] [8♣♣] [7♦♦] [2♣]

beats [A♠] [8♣♣] [7♦♦] [3♦♦] [2♦♦]

LIMITS FOR BEGINNERS

Now that you know how to bet, let's talk for a minute
about *how much* you can bet.

"Ring" games, a fancy term for a normal poker game (as
opposed to a tournament), come in three basic flavors:
structured limit, **no-limit**, and **pot-limit**.

If you're new to the game, you're going to want to stick to
a structured limit game, that is, one where the size of the bet
is fixed on each street. For example, in a "$5/10" hold'em
game, the bets (or raises) are made in increments of $5
before and just after the flop—the **small bet**—but increase
to units of $10 on the turn and the river—the **big bet**.

A no-limit game is exactly what the name suggests, a game in which there's no limit to the amount that you can bet at any time. (Note that there is often a minimum size for each bet or raise.) Many online and casino no-limit games have a maximum buy-in, such as $50 or $500. This helps to prevent one player from steamrolling over everyone else simply by virtue of starting with a much larger **stack** of chips. Any chips that you earn above and beyond the buy-in, however, can be used to bully new players at will.

Pot-limit is a sophisticated hybrid of the two in which you can make a maximum bet at any time of up to the amount of money that is currently in the pot. It's a lot trickier than it sounds. Suffice to say here that there's a galaxy of difference between a $5/10 limit hold'em game (where pots can get into the low hundreds) and a $5/10 pot-limit game (where those same pots can climb into the thousands).

♥ ♦ ♣ ♠ ♥ ♦ ♣ ♠ ♥ ♦ ♣ ♠ ♥ ♦ ♣ ♠ ♥ ♦ ♣ ♠ ♥ ♦ ♣ ♠ ♥ ♦ ♣ ♠

YOUR DEFINING MOMENT

You're out at the local Hallmark store picking up a Get Well Soon card for your sick grandmother. After taking a wrong turn at the fake Lladro figurines, you find yourself smack dab in front of a display of Kem Cards. The $19.99 price tag seems a bit high for a couple of cut-up sheets of plastic, but you just won $25 on a scratch-off lottery ticket. You decide to take the plunge. Your life will never be the same.

When you get home, you cut the cellophane and take the cards out of the box. You begin to shuffle. You're a natural. Getting a little cocky, you go for "the bridge." The cards slip from your hands, flying wildly around the room.

What happens next is a miracle—as the cards land on the floor, most of them group together in clusters of seven. Recognizing this as a training opportunity courtesy of the poker gods, you organize each cluster of cards into the best possible five-card hand . . .

Cluster #1:

| 2♥ | 7♥ | 3♦ | 3♣ | A♦ | 4♥ | 5♣ |

Cluster #2:

| 2♣ | 2♦ | 2♠ | 9♣ | 9♥ | 5♥ | 5♠ |

Cluster #3:

| 4♠ | 6♠ | A♣ | Q♦ | 10♠ | K♥ | J♠ |

Cluster #4:

| J♥ | 9♦ | 10♣ | J♦ | 8♥ | J♦ | 7♣ |

Cluster #5:

| 3♠ | 3♥ | A♠ | 4♦ | 6♥ | 6♣ | 4♣ |

Cluster #6:

| Q♦ | K♣ | K♦ | Q♠ | Q♥ | 8♣ | K♠ |

Cluster #7:

| 10♦ | 5♦ | A♦ | 7♦ | 6♦ | 9♠ | 8♦ |

Extra Credit:

Which of the hands above could be improved by replacing one of its cards with one of the three leftover cards?

| 7♠ | 8♠ | 10♥ |

THE ANSWERS

Cluster #1:

Straight (an ace-to-five straight is called a "bicycle")

| A♦ | 2♥ ♥ | 3♦ ♦ | 4♣ ♣ | 5♣ ♣ |

Cluster #2:

Full House ("twos full of nines")

| 2♣ ♣ | 2♦ ♦ | 2♠ ♠ | 9♣ ♣ | 9♥ ♥ |

Cluster #3:

Queen-High Flush

| Q♠ | J♠ | 10♠ ♠ | 6♠ ♠ | 4♠ ♠ |

Cluster #4:

Jack-High Straight

| 7♣ ♣ | 8♠ ♠ | 9♦ ♦ | 10♣ ♣ | J♥ |

Cluster #5:

Two Pair ("sixes over fours with an ace **kicker**")

| 6♥ ♥ | 6♣ ♣ | 4♦ ♦ | 4♣ ♣ | A♠ |

Cluster #6:

Full House ("kings full of queens")

| Q♦ | K♣ | K♦ | K♠ | Q♥ | Q♦ |

Cluster #7:

Ace-High Flush (but *almost* a Straight Flush)

| A♦ | 10♦ ♦ | 8♦ ♦ | 7♦ ♦ | 6♦ ♦ |

Extra Credit:

Cluster #4—replace the 9♦ ♦ with any of the discards to make a Full House. Or Cluster #3—replace the 6♠ ♠ or 4♠ ♠ with the 7♠ ♠ or 8♠ ♠ to get a higher flush.

3

THE FIRST DAY OF SCHOOL

You'll practice your grip on the cards; what's important is that you've developed a grip on the basics. You're ready to play the damn game.

Only you don't want to just play: You want to win.

As you sit at the lunch counter poring over the pages of this book, a fellow diner shoots you a cynical look. "What's the point of reading a book about poker? I thought it was all about luck."

Well, he's right. A poker player has to be lucky—in the same way that Warren Buffet gets lucky playing the stock market year after year.

When played "correctly"—with the intention of winning

money—poker is a lot like value investing. You bet heavily on hands that you have a better than average chance of winning, and you minimize your outlay for those that you don't.

So while poker does ultimately come down to luck, there's absolutely nothing to prevent an educated player from taking advantage of fortune's ups and downs.

The concepts that follow represent the cornerstone of a poker education, beginning with a few more myths that have to be dispelled.

"ANY TWO CARDS CAN WIN!"

Getting dealt a seven and a deuce of different suits—a hand we'll call 7-2 offsuit, or 7-2o for short—might not seem as glamorous as "waking up" with pocket aces. But if the flop comes 7-7-2, you are looking at a **monster**. You've got to play everything, because you never know what the flop will bring. Any two cards can win!

You'll hear this cry often, especially at poker's lower limits. And here's a little secret . . . it's true!

Well, it's technically true, anyway. A much deeper truth is this: While any two cards can win, some combinations win a lot more often than others.

Go back to the example above. The player holding 7-2o needs a 7 or a 2 to make a pair. Neither of those pairs alone would be good enough to beat a hand like a pair of aces; to win, this player is actually going to have to make at least two pair or three of a kind while hoping the aces don't improve.

The player with pocket aces, on the other hand, doesn't

need to improve at all. All he or she has to hope for is that the player with 7-2o doesn't get lucky.

Make that *really* lucky—in a **heads-up** showdown, pocket aces will make the better hand around 88 percent of the time.*

Poker, especially limit poker, is a game of **expected value**. You win money by betting in situations in which you have a positive expected value, and holding on to it when your expected value is negative.

This may sound like a tricky mathematical concept, but it's actually pretty easy. Let's say that you find yourself in an A-A vs. 7-2o showdown one hundred times. To keep it simple, let's say each player bets $5 each time, for a total of $10 in each pot. Over the course of a hundred hands, each of you will have wagered $500 ($5 x 100 hands), or $1,000 total.

The person with A-A can expect to win 88 percent of the time, or 88 of the 100 times. Each pot is $10, so the person with **wired** aces should win around $880. That's a $380 profit: $880 in winnings minus the $500 you've contributed to the hundred pots. In other words, the aces have a very healthy positive expected value. The player with 7-2o, on the other hand, will only win the remaining 12 out of 100 times, raking in a total of $120. Subtract the $500 invested, and this player is looking at a $380 *loss,* an unseemly negative expected value.

The first secret to winning hold'em, therefore, is to learn which hands have positive expected value. This is a skill called **hand selection**.

---

* Don't worry about how those odds were calculated—it's damn near impossible to figure out without a "poker calculator." You can find poker calculators on the Web; *Cardplayer* magazine offers a particularly good one at *www.cardplayer.com.*

SOME PERCENTAGES

If you have a pocket pair, you'll flop a set about 12 percent of the time.

If you have A-K, you'll flop at least a pair about 37 percent of the time.

If you have two suited cards, you will flop four cards to a flush about 11 percent of the time.

What makes some hands better than others? Taking a lesson from the example, it's clear that pocket pairs, especially big ones, can be very powerful, as they can win without any extra help from the board. When they do match up with the community cards, they'll make brawny hands like sets and full houses. Higher cards are better than lower ones, as they make bigger hands (with bigger kickers). Cards that are of the same suit—a condition we'll call **suited**—have a better chance of making flushes, while consecutive (or near-consecutive) cards—**connectors**—are more likely to make straights. **Suited connectors** are even better, increasing your odds of making a straight, flush or, on rare occasions, a straight flush. Hands that incorporate both hole cards are generally stronger than hands that use only one, as you're less likely to end up in a tie with an opponent, forcing you to split the pot.

HOLD'EM POKER FOR ADVANCED PLAYERS
by David Sklansky and Mason Malmuth

No poker library would be complete without this book, arguably the most powerful text ever written on Texas Hold'em.

It can be an infuriating book to read. Sklansky (who you should recognize as one of the contributors to *Super/System*) and Malmuth are men of mathematics, not, as they readily admit, masters of clear communication. Even if you're hip to scientific language, the book offers so much so fast that it can take multiple readings to digest some of the concepts within.

But oh, what concepts they are. During the course of your poker career, you will frequently make astounding discoveries at the table—a novel new way, perhaps, to handle a particular situation—only to find out later that Sklansky and Malmuth had addressed that very situation in a seemingly tossed-off line you managed to completely overlook during your previous readings.

The book's greatest claim to fame might be found in its first few pages, a chart ranking what Sklansky and Malmuth have determined to be the seventy or so "playable" hold'em hands. Pocket aces sit mightily at the top of the heap, while the much humbler 10-8o dwells in the cellar. (That 7-2o of the earlier example—the absolute worst hand in hold'em as it can't use both cards to make a straight or a flush—doesn't make the cut.)

Sklansky and Malmuth break these hands down into eight separate groups, from best to worst, reprinted here with the permission of the authors and Two Plus Two Publishing LLC:

Group 1: A-A, K-K, Q-Q, J-J, A-Ks*

Group 2: 10-10, A-Qs, A-Js, K-Qs, A-K

Group 3: 9-9, J-10s, Q-Js, K-Js, A-10s, A-Q

Group 4: 10-9s, K-Q, 8-8, Q-10s, 9-8s, J-9s, A-J, K-10s

Group 5: 7-7, 8-7s, Q-9s, 10-8s, K-J, Q-J, J-10, 7-6s, 9-7s, A-xs, 6-5s

Group 6: 6-6, A-10, 5-5, 8-6s, K-10, Q-10, 5-4s, K-9s, J-8s, 7-5s

Group 7: 4-4, J-9, 6-4s, 10-9, 5-3s, 3-3, 9-8, 4-3s, 2-2, K-xs, 10-7s, Q-8s

Group 8: 8-7, A-9, Q-9, 7-6, 4-2s, 3-2s, 9-6s, 8-5s, J-8, J-7s, 6-5, 5-4, 7-4s, K-9, 10-8

These rankings have engendered some controversy over the years as critics, often armed with computer simulations, quibble over the values assigned to certain hands. Anyone who regularly watches the professional game will see hands played that, somehow, Sklansky and Malmuth managed to overlook, such as the 10-2 that Doyle Brunson used to win both of his World Series bracelets.

There's no denying, however, that this is *the* list by which all others are judged. Every serious poker player has committed these hand rankings to memory.

---

* The "s" signifies two cards of the same suit, while "x" indicates any small card. "A-xs," therefore, means an ace with a smaller card of the same suit.

"NEVER DRAW FOR AN INSIDE STRAIGHT"

Everybody knows that drawing to an inside straight is a sucker's play. There's only one card in the deck (well, four cards, to be precise) that can help you.

Or can they?

In most cases, if you're going to draw at a straight, you should at least be **open-ended**—

You   The Board

(any ace or nine will save you)

—or on a **double belly-buster**—

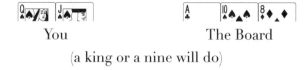

You   The Board

(a king or a nine will do)

Draws—those hands where you decide to stick around for another bet or two in the hopes of improving—are the reason so many poker players suffer from something akin to bipolar disorder. Spike a big draw on the river, and you'll smile as you rake in a very big pot. Chase and miss, however, and you've paid an expensive price for a whole lot of misery.

So when is it right to draw? Same as when it's correct to play a hand: when the expected value of betting that hand is positive. What's different, however, is that you don't need a poker calculator to do the computations. A third-grade math education will do.

Let's use a simple coin flip as an example. You have a

50 percent chance of flipping heads. But what are the odds *against* flipping heads? Well, if you flip that coin one hundred times, the results should be somewhere in the neighborhood of fifty heads and fifty tails. Your odds against flipping heads are 50 to 50, or 1-to-1.

Gamblers like odds, because they quickly indicate whether or not a wager has a positive expectation. If the odds against flipping heads are 1-to-1, you'd want to be getting (at least) odds of 1-to-1 on your money, or a dollar paid for a dollar risked. After 100 flips of the coin, you will have made $50 for the times you made heads, but you'll have lost $50 on those instances when the coin came up tails. A break-even proposition.

Now let's say that your grandmother, after one martini too many, offers you 2-to-1 odds on that same coin flip. In other words, she'll pay you $2 every time you win, but only take $1 each time you lose. After 100 flips of the coin, you'll still have forked over $50 for all of the tails, but you'll have won $100 for the heads. You should be able to take the hapless matron for somewhere in the neighborhood of $50.

This concept makes its way into poker in the form of pot odds. If there's $40 in the pot, and a $10 bet in front of you, the pot is laying you odds of $40 to $10, or 4-to-1. As you might expect, you are getting the correct pot odds to call a bet as long as your odds of making the best hand are 4-to-1 or better.

Okay, this part is a little tricky: You're getting "4-to-1 odds" on your draw when you have a hand that will miss four times for every one time that it hits. In other words, a hand with 4-to-1 odds is a hand that you'll hit once in every *five* tries.

Think about it in terms of the pot. If there's $40 in the pot, and it's costing you $10 to call, how often do you need to succeed? You can miss four times—that will cost you $40—but if you hit it the fifth time, you'll win the $40 pot (plus the $10 you risked) and come out even.

Let this settle in for a minute: It's the toughest mathematical concept you'll have to master in order to be a winning poker player. When you talk about a hand that's getting 4-to-1 odds on a draw, what you are really saying is that you are going to complete that draw one time in five, or 20 percent of the time.

So how do you know if your hand will win 20 percent of the time? You start by determining which cards can help you make your hand. Poker players call these **outs**.

Go back to the two straight draws at the beginning of this section. In each case, two different cards would make your hand. Each of those cards comes in four different suits, making eight cards in all that can help you. In other words, you have eight outs to your straight.

Okay, now what? Well, that depends on how much you like math. If you're well versed in the laws of statistical probability, feel free to run through four or so steps of calculation required to determine an accurate answer. If you're just looking for a quick estimate—which is all you'll need in most cases—use the **rule of four**: Multiply the number of outs by four, and you'll have a rough approximation of your chances of completing your hand with two cards (the turn and the river) to come. In this case, with eight outs, you have about a 32 percent chance of making your hand.

Now we have to figure out the odds. If you're going to win this scenario 32 percent of the time (32/100, or about once in every three times), then you are going to lose 68 percent of the time (about two out of every three times). Your odds of making the straight, therefore, are approximately 2-to-1 against.

So should you chase your eight-outer? Yes, as long as the pot contains $2 for every $1 you have to wager.

One final word on odds: The rule of four is used to calculate the odds of making your hand with *two* cards to come, the turn and the river. You may have noticed an implication here: You may have to call not just one, but *two* bets, in order to see a river card. Doesn't this screw up our analysis of pot odds?

The simple answer—yes, it does. Do you have to worry about it? Not very often, thanks to a concept called **implied pot odds**. This is basically a fancy way of saying that, before the hand is over, the pot is going to grow even larger. In most cases, if you're getting the right odds to pay to see the turn card, you're going to be getting the right odds to fork over a second bet to see the river. If you ever find yourself doubting the wisdom of making a particular bet, you can multiply your number of outs by *two* instead of four, giving you a rough approximation of your chances of making the hand with one card to come instead of two.

In truth, this is a gross oversimplification of implied pot odds. For a far more thorough treatment, you'd do well to read *The Theory of Poker* (see below).

The good news—this is the last math lesson in the book. As a reward for getting through it, here's a useful tip:

The larger the pot, the more inclined you should be to win it as quickly as possible.

The reasoning behind this is simple once you've grasped the concept of pot odds. Decent-sized pots generally provide correct odds for your opponents to call bets with their open-ended straights or four-card flushes. Once a pot gets large, however, your opponents will have the right odds to draw for all kinds of hands. Eleven-to-one odds are enough to make it okay to break that cardinal rule and draw for the inside straight. A huge pot—capped before the flop—may give your opponents good reason to draw with unimproved pocket pairs (looking for the two outs that will make them a set) or even **backdoor flushes**.

Nip these speculators in their respective buds by taking down those pots before the odds get crazy enough for them to start acting crazy. We'll get to the tools that will help you accomplish this in the next section.

THE THEORY OF POKER

by David Sklansky

The guy didn't earn the nickname "Einstein" for nothing. No one has contributed more to the study of the scientific principles governing poker than David Sklansky.

The Theory of Poker is his masterpiece. He covers, from the ground up, everything you need to know about the mathematics of odds, implied odds, check-

THE FIRST DAY OF SCHOOL

raising, even bluffing. Perhaps his most brilliant stroke is the Fundamental Theorem of Poker:

Every time you play a hand differently from the way you would have played it if you could see all your opponents' cards, they gain; and every time you play your hand the same way you would have played it if you could see all their cards, they lose. Conversely, every time opponents play their hands differently from the way they would have if they could see all your cards, they gain; and every time they play their hands the same way they would have played if they could see all your cards, you lose.

Okay, poetry it's not. But powerful, powerful stuff. *The Theory of Poker* belongs on every poker player's bookshelf.

"THE DEAL IS OF NO SPECIAL VALUE"

The next myth to be dispelled is from a pamphlet on poker, written in the late nineteenth century by General Robert Schenck, the American ambassador to England, who intended to teach the finer points of the game to a British duchess. Whatever other virtues General Schenck might have possessed, he was dead wrong about the value of being the dealer.

In the example presented earlier, pocket aces worked very effectively in a heads-up battle against one other player. Hold'em, however, is a game that's usually dealt nine- or ten-handed. Most of the time—especially early in your poker career—you will be up against more than one player. Where you act in relation to these other players— your **position**—is extremely important. And as you might remember from the previous chapter, the player seated in the dealer position gets to act last during every round of betting from the flop on.

Why is this so important? For the simple reason that you get to see what everyone else is up to before having to commit any money yourself. If there's a lot of raising or re-raising in front of you, it might be wise to fold your hand. If everyone checks to you, a bluff at the pot might be in order.

Relative position is a critical factor in determining just how strong a hand you are holding. Some hands that might initially seem valuable are actually very difficult to play if you have to decide whether to check, bet, or fold before a large field of other players who are set to act.

Before the flop, your position at the table is usually broken down into four basic categories:

1. **Early Position** (EP). The two or three players seated directly to the left of the blinds have to decide before anyone else does whether or not to enter—or raise—the pot. There could be a lot of scary hands out there. (The player in first position is said to be under the gun for this very reason.) It's usually wise, therefore, to limit yourself to the stronger hands of the hold'em spectrum.

2. **Middle Position** (MP). The three or four players in the middle have an easier time of it. They get to see what the EPs do before the flop, and won't have to make any decisions after the flop until the blinds and EPs have acted. It's a luxury that allows you to play a relatively wider selection of hands. If no one has entered the pot

before you, you can think about raising with some of the hands you might have thrown away from early position. And if an EP has already raised, you can safely fold some of your marginal holdings.

3. **Late Position** (LP). This is the area some poker players like to call "the office," as it's the best place from which to do your work at the table. The crown jewel of late position is the **button**, or the dealer's seat. As the button, you not only get to act last on every round of betting after the flop, but if no one has entered the pot before you, you can try to **steal the blinds**, raising with a hand that wouldn't ordinarily be worth two bets in the hopes of scaring the blinds into folding.

4. The **Small** and **Big Blinds** (SB & BB). These may be the trickiest positions to play well in Texas Hold'em. It might seem like a great seat before the flop: Not only do you get to act last, but you get to enter the pot at a discount (since you've already posted a bet or a fraction of a bet), giving you the right odds to play many weaker-than-usual hands. After the flop, however, the blinds are obligated to act first on every round, making it extremely dangerous to play those weaker hands.

As a basic rule of thumb, you generally don't want to play anything from early position worse than what Sklansky and Malmuth call a Group 4. Playing hands from Group 5 or 6 is usually okay from middle position. Hands from Group 7 and 8 are best played, if at all, from late position or for a fractional bet from the blinds.

This rule of thumb, however, greatly depends on how your opponents play. Against very aggressive competition, you'll want to "tighten up," limiting yourself to better hands. Some hands, like small pocket pairs and suited connectors, do better against large fields of opponents, for reasons that will become evident later in this chapter.

Learning the right time and place to play certain hands is one of poker's never-ending challenges.

POSITION, POSITION, POSITION

Here's an experiment to try if you're already playing online poker: Log onto the site and join a very low-limit game—a 5¢/10¢ table will do just fine. Now put a strip of black tape on your monitor, covering your hole cards.

If players seem to be raising too many pots, re-raise from late position. If they are playing in a very straightforward manner—betting if they've connected with the flop, checking if they've missed—call them when you're in late position. Once the flop comes down, you can fold when they bet and bet when they don't. If you pay careful attention to the way the other players are betting and use your position "correctly" (i.e., in a way that maximizes its value), you may be able to beat this game, even without ever seeing your own cards!

"THERE'S NO POINT IN RAISING UNTIL YOU SEE THE FLOP"

Ace-king, or as poker players call it, **Big Slick**, is a very powerful hand. Flop an ace or a king, and you've not only got the top pair, but the best possible kicker to boot. A straight made with Big Slick is a nut straight—someone's going to need a flush or better to beat you. Ace-king, almost every poker book will tell you, is a hand you raise with before the flop.

Over half of the time you play Big Slick, however, the flop is going to miss you completely. You'll often see people at the table who, after playing ace-king "by the book," shake their head in disgust at a jack-high flop, wondering why they bothered raising with it in the first place. Wouldn't it have been smarter just to have **limped** in? Some players will tell you that they *never* raise before the flop with Big Slick—why waste extra money before you've seen a flop?

Once again, there's more to this story. Here are some very good reasons for raising before the flop:

1. **You have a strong hand.** If you knew a particular stock was likely to outperform some of the others in your portfolio, you'd want to invest more of your money in its shares. The same thinking applies to **premium hands**, especially those in Group One—you may not win with them all of the time, but they'll certainly make the best hand more often than almost any other holding. Take advantage of the "investment opportunity" and get more money into the pot.

2. **You want to narrow the field.** Pocket aces will beat almost any other hand, in a one-on-one contest, about 80 percent

of the time. Against two opponents, however, their dominance shrinks to just over 70 percent—there are more ways for someone to connect strongly with the board. Put those aces up against several opponents, and the odds of winning may drop to less than 50 percent. When you raise (or re-raise) before the flop, you'll often scare off some players who would have called a single bet, limiting the number of players involved in a pot, increasing your chances of winning. There is also a possibility of knocking everyone out of the hand before it starts, winning the blinds without a contest. Remember that it's always better to win a small pot than to lose a big one.

3. **You want to isolate a weaker opponent.** If a single player, who you know will limp in (or even raise) with all kinds of less-than-playable hands, has entered the pot, and you estimate that a raise (or a re-raise) has a good chance of knocking out all of the players behind you, it's often a good idea to fire away with any better-than-average hand. If it works, you'll find yourself heads-up against the weak player with advantageous position throughout.

4. **All the players in front of you have folded.** It's usually tough to decide on a course of action from early position, as there are still a lot of players left to act, some of whom could wake up with very strong hands. As the players in front of you fold, however, the odds of your hand being the best hand start to increase. It's often good poker, if you find yourself the first person to act, to raise with hands in late position that you wouldn't consider playing under the gun.

5. **You want your opponents to think you have a strong hand.** The effects of a **pre-flop** raise aren't limited to the opponents you scare off—your early display of strength encourages your opponents to tread lightly after the flop. They might check in situations where they would ordinarily bet, and fold in those where they might call. In a point we'll make throughout the book, poker rewards aggression, and there's no more aggressive statement you can make before the flop than coming in with a raise.

It's almost always a good idea to raise (and, very often, to re-raise) before the flop with a Group One hand. The better your position, the wider the range of hands you can consider raising with. If everyone's folded to you on the button, for example, you can raise with just about anything you think has a better-than-average chance of winning.

However, there are also times where you should be less inclined to throw in a pre-flop raise:

1. **Someone else has already raised.** Unless you've got a great read on an opponent's style of play, it's a good idea to take his or her raises seriously. Many professional players' default response to a pre-flop raise is to look for a reason to fold.

2. **You don't want to narrow the field.** Connectors and suited cards are generally considered **drawing hands**. In other words, you have a much better chance of flopping cards that will get you part of the way to a flush or a straight than you do of flopping a made hand: You're going to have to "draw" cards on the turn, and the possibly the river, in the hopes of getting there. These are more speculative investments, meaning you want to risk less up front while keeping more of your opponents involved, aiming for a bigger-than-normal reward should you make your hand. We'll get into how to evaluate these kinds of situations in the next section.

3. **Your raises aren't working.** Very often—especially early in your poker career, amidst the bloody mayhem of "No Fold'em Hold'em"—you'll find yourself at a table where your raises seem to do the opposite of what you intended. Not only will your opponents refuse to respect the authority of your double-bet, but they'll trip over one another in their hurry to get their money into the growing pot, sometimes raising, re-raising, and **capping** the betting in the hopes of creating an enormous payday. Enormous pots can be problematic: They create incentive for players to hang around until the end with all kinds of otherwise

unlikely propositions. A table full of people drawing on unlikely propositions is likely to result in a gut-wrenching defeat. In these wild games, it *is* often a good idea to wait until you see the flop before investing too much money into the hand.

THE WHEN, THE WHY, AND THE HOW OF POKER

So far, this chapter has been focused on the "When" of poker. When should I play a hand? When should I chase a draw? When should I fold?

Understanding the When of poker is like a toddler learning right from wrong. It's an essential building block of any player's education.

There comes a point, however, when that toddler is going to ask "Why?" A complicated question in the real world, to be sure, but a relatively easy question to answer at the poker table:

To win, on the hands that you win, as much money as possible, and to lose, on the hands that you lose, as little money as possible.

Reread the previous sentence. Let it settle in. This is the Why of poker.

Simple advice, right? You'd be amazed at how many of your opponents will ignore it. (We'll get into some of the other motivations that drive these players in Chapter Six.)

Now that you have a grasp on the When and the Why, you're ready to take on the How.

THE TOOLBOX

Every carpenter uses a hammer and nails. No plumber is without a selection of wrenches. Poker players have their own set of tools. Some are certainly more powerful than others, but there's a time to use each of them. The How of poker is accomplished by knowing which tool will best suit the particular task in front of you.

FOLDING

This is the flathead screwdriver in your box, the tool you'll use most often. At a full table, you'll probably be folding at least two out of every three hands before the flop, and a significant percentage of your hands once you see (and fail to connect with) those first three cards.

Many of your opponents will perceive folding as a sign of weakness, or of your being an all-around tight-ass. They're wrong (about the weakness, anyway)—folding is probably the most powerful tool at your disposal.

Remember the Why of poker. You're looking not just to maximize the amount that you win, but to *minimize what you lose.* Nothing accomplishes that better than folding your hand and waiting for a better spot to play. Find the love of folding, and you'll discover its rewards will be plentiful.

BETTING AND RAISING

At the risk of stretching the metaphor thin, these are your power tools. If your hand is good enough to call a bet, you should strongly consider betting yourself. If you were thinking about betting, and someone's beat you to it, give serious thought to raising.

Betting or raising is almost always superior to just calling. When you call, you have only one way to win: Your hand has to be the best hand. Bet or raise, however, and there are suddenly two ways to come out on top: Your opponent may fold (sometimes, on your better days, with a hand that's got you beat); and even if he doesn't, you may wind up with the best hand.

This is the tool you use when the situation requires aggression, a mind-set that poker has a funny way of rewarding (more on this in Chapter Five).

CHECKING AND CALLING

This is the weakest tool in your kit. There are all kinds of nicknames for players who check and call too much, including **ATM**, **fish**, and **pigeon**. Almost every poker book you read will have something negative to say about calling. "Raise or fold" is a mantra for many winning players.

That being said, it's a tool that does have its uses. Let's say the flop hits you, but weakly—maybe you have top pair with a weak kicker. Or the board looks like it could have made a flush or a straight for someone other than you. If there are several players to act behind you, discretion should be your watchword. Wait and see what everyone else does before committing any money to the pot.

If you are on the come, drawing to a better hand (with the correct pot odds, of course) against opponents who are unlikely to fold to your bet or raise, calling is usually the proper course of action.

It's also occasionally correct to just check and call against superaggressive opponents who like to push their mediocre holdings or flat-out bluff. This is especially true on the river, when, if you think there's any chance of your hand being the best hand, it's almost always worth calling a bet. (Think about it in terms of pot odds: You generally only have to be "right" a small percentage of the time for this to be a profitable play.)

Checking and calling on the river can also be a good way to induce a bluff from your opponent. A good rule of thumb: *If the only way your opponent can call your bet is if he or she has got you beat, then it's usually better to check and call.*

For example, say you hold J♥ 10♦ and the board is

J♣ 7♥ 6♥ 4♥ 3♥

Your jack-high flush may very well be the best hand, but it's unlikely that your opponent would call a bet with a hand that's worse than yours. If you check, an aggressive player might believe that you don't have a heart and bet into you. You'll win an extra bet if your hand is good, and you've saved yourself from having to call your opponent's likely raise should your hand be second best.

BLUFFING

To the uninitiated, poker is all about bluffing. Consider this your initiation—they are wrong! While bluffing is certainly an important part of the game, it's not as effective a play as you may have been led to believe.

In order for a bluff to work, you have to be using it against an opponent who is scared enough or, more importantly, *smart* enough to fold. This is the "Paradox of the Bluff": It's a terrible play to make against terrible opponents.

Limit poker—especially the lower limits—is a show-down game, meaning you very often have to show the best hand to win a pot. Lots of players see flops, and many of them won't be savvy enough to recognize when you have them dominated, let alone when you are *pretending* to have them dominated. *Bluffing in a typical low-limit poker game is generally a complete waste of time—and money.*

When you do bluff, you'd prefer to be doing it against as few opponents as possible—one is best—minimizing the chances that someone has a hand that they *just have to call you* with. It's pretty pointless to bluff against maniacs or morons, so limit the play to your opponents who show weakness, or at least some sign of paying attention to the way you conduct yourself at the table.

One good time to bluff is when a **scare card** appears on the board. For example, say you call a raise from the blind with 10♥ 9♥, and the flop comes

J♥ 6♠ 2♦

You check to Raising Ray, who also checks. You've been watching Ray long enough to guess that he's probably got a hand like ace-king or ace-queen, but is afraid that you might have connected with the board. Now the turn card is the J♠. This is a very scary card for Ray—he has no way of knowing that he's got the best hand—and represents a great situation to bluff at the pot.

Your bluffs don't have to work every time to have a positive expectation—one success can more than make up for three or four failures. It's also not a bad idea to get caught bluffing every once in a while, as your opponents will be more likely to give you action the next time you actually hold a legitimate hand.

SEMI-BLUFFING

A **semi-bluff** is a bet or a raise made with a hand that, while not currently the best, has a chance of getting there. If your opponents fold, fantastic; if they don't, you still have a decent shot of drawing to a winning hand.

Semi-bluffing is most often used to get a "free card" on a more expensive street. For example, let's say you're dealt A♣ K♣ on the button. A player in early position limps in. You raise. The Big Blind and the early position player—let's call her Limping Lucy—both call. Now the flop comes . . .

. . . and Lucy bets into you. This is a great time for a semi-bluff raise. While she may very well have a better hand than you at the moment, you have nine outs to a nut flush, plus another six outs to an ace or a king that might also make you the best hand. Your raise will probably encourage the Big Blind, confronted with a double-sized bet, to fold, and you may scare Lucy off as well. Even if she calls, she'll likely check to you on the turn. If the turn card makes your hand, you can go ahead and bet it. If it doesn't, you can check behind her, getting a "free" look at the river card.

In other words, by investing an extra small bet on the flop, you've saved yourself from having to call a big bet on the turn. Note that for this play to be effective, you have to be in later position than the original bettor—one more example of how important having good position is to a skilled poker player.

Also keep in mind that many veteran players are hip to the old semi-bluff for a free card, and may re-raise you and bet into you on the turn, nullifying the "discount" you were looking for.

CHECK-RAISING

As the name suggests, the move involves checking in front of an opponent or opponents in the hope that one (or more) of them makes a bet. When the action gets back to you, you raise. It's generally a good idea to be holding a very strong hand when you do, as many players like to call down check-raisers "just to see," and the increased money in the pot can sometimes create situations where it becomes correct for your opponents to call with all kinds of crazy draws.

The play has endured some criticism over the years—some players of old believed that this particular type of duplicity constituted bad manners—but in today's game, the check-raise is an undeniably valuable tool, helping you to extract the most money possible with your winning hands. It also may be one of the most overused.

You have to be very confident that someone is going to bet behind you. If no one takes the bait, not only have you failed to make any money from this particular street, but you've given all of your opponents a dreaded free card, possibly allowing them to draw out on you. When in doubt, it's almost always better just to bet your stronger hands.

Check-raising is most effective against one other opponent, especially when a seemingly innocuous card has helped you, or when you want to "clear the field" with a double-bet.

For example, let's say you call from early position with

[10♣] [10♥]. Limping Lucy, seated in middle position, calls behind you, before Raising Ray ups it to two bets from the button. The blinds fold; Lucy calls. Now the flop comes . . .

[K♠] [10♦] [9♣]

Your set of tens is probably in the lead right now. Rather than betting out, however, the wiser play is to check to Raising Ray, who seems likely to bet, then raise when the action gets back to you. Not only will you get more money into the pot, but by confronting Lucy with a double-sized bet, you may get her to throw away a potentially danger-ous hand that otherwise might have been worth a call, like [K♦] [J♦] or [Q♣] [10♠].

SLOWPLAYING

Sometimes a flop hits you so hard and looks so menacing that any aggression on your part will scare off your oppo-nents. By **slowplaying**, or passively checking and calling on the early streets, you can sometimes lure opponents into making ill-advised bets and raises on the later, more expensive streets.

This is the tool most abused by new poker players, who fall in love with the idea of being able to trap their opponents.* For one thing, it's always dangerous to give free cards—very few hands are such absolute locks that your opponents will be **drawing dead.** Secondly, your opponents are often more

* **Fancy Play Syndrome**, or FPS, is a condition that afflicts many new (and quite a few experienced) players. Its primary symptoms are the overuse of the more specialized tools like check-raising and slowplaying, missing opportunities to extract extra bets while giving potentially dangerous free cards to their opponents. Straightforward poker—betting when you have the best hand, folding when you don't—may seem boring, but it's generally the most profitable way to play the game.

likely to call a bet on the flop than on the more expensive turn or river, meaning that you may be sacrificing your only opportunity to milk any money out of them.

The best time to slowplay is when your hand is not only a cinch or near-cinch to win, but when allowing your opponents to take a free card offers a decent chance of making them a *second-best hand.*

For example, say you're dealt 4♣ 4♦ in late position. Limping Lucy calls in front of you. You raise. Both the blinds call. So does Lucy. The flop comes

10♥ 4♠ 4♥

You have four of a kind, virtually unbeatable. Everyone checks to you. A bet here will likely win the pot. Check, however, and all kinds of good things might happen to you on fourth street. Maybe Lucy, who was afraid to bet into the flop with her 10♣ 9♦ , finds the courage to take a stab. An ace or king may give someone a big pair. On your best days, the turn card winds up making a flush for one opponent and a full house for another, setting up a raising war from which you will come away victorious— and substantially wealthier.

Before moving on, take note of how specific these conditions were. If the flop had instead come . . .

10♥ 9♠ 4♥

. . . granting a free card to your opponents would be a terrible mistake, as trip fours are dog meat should someone make a straight or a flush.

WINNING LOW-LIMIT HOLD'EM

by Lee Jones

Who is Lee Jones? A great tournament champion? A fearless competitor in ultra-high-stakes cash games? A genius in the mathematics of poker?

The answer is (d), none of the above. He's a computer programmer from San Jose, California, who happened to write an incredibly useful book for poker newbies.

While there's no denying the genius of Sklansky and Malmuth, their works presuppose that your level of competition has some sense of how to play the game.* Unfortunately, your early sorties at the poker table will likely pit you against people who, to put it nicely, don't have a clue. They will play too many hands. They won't know when to fold. They will make all kinds of "mistakes" that can actually wind up costing *you* a lot of money if you aren't prepared for them.

Jones puts a lot of emphasis on "reading the board." To succeed at low-limit poker, you've got to examine a flop with the idea that one or more opponents have already made some kind of hand, or at least picked up a draw. His book helps you learn how to value your hand in relation to the cards that are out there, enabling you

---

* In response to the growing popularity of the low-limit game, Sklansky and Malmuth recently teamed with one Ed Miller to release a book called *Small Stakes Hold 'em: Winning Big with Expert Play*.

to make better decisions about when and how to proceed.

While *Winning Low-Limit Hold'em* shouldn't be the last book you read on poker, you could do a lot worse than making it one of the first.

OTHER FORMS OF PRACTICE

If you're looking to hone your skills before testing them out on a live opponent, you might find it helpful to get some practice against a simulator.

There are all kinds of computer simulations out there, from virtual casinos to small applets you can play on your Palm Pilot. Unfortunately, most computers generally don't play a very good game of Texas Hold'em (see page 61).

The best of the bunch seem to be the "Turbo" series of programs developed by Bob Wilson, poker player, software entrepreneur, and longtime member of Mensa. The artificial intelligence governing the play is pretty good, and a fairly sophisticated set of controls allow you to customize the individual playing style of each virtual opponent you'll face. The Wilson programs are expensive—they currently retail for about $90 a pop—but his Web site (*www.wilsonsoftware.com*) is full of testimonials from real people promising that you'll quickly recoup the investment through your improved play.

THE COMPUTER HAND

It's another one of those stories that reeks of being anecdotal, but it has managed to linger around long enough to earn its own place in poker lore. Apparently someone, somewhere, at some time, ran a computer simulation to see which hands in Texas Hold'em were worth playing. As the legend goes, this computer revealed that Q-7 was the worst of the profitable hands.

In actuality, Q-7—which still carries the nickname of "the computer hand"—is a pretty awful holding, and there's not a winning poker player in the world who would play it with any regularity. The story does, however, illuminate the difficulties of using computers to figure things out about poker, a game that's perhaps a little too nuanced for our current crop of machines.

♥ ♦ ♣ ♠ ♥ ♦ ♣ ♠ ♥ ♦ ♣ ♠ ♥ ♦ ♣ ♠ ♥ ♦ ♣ ♠ ♥ ♦ ♣ ♠

YOUR DEFINING MOMENT

You're playing Texas Hold'em for nickel blinds against your grandmother (she's feeling better), who has been carving you to pieces with her relentlessly aggressive play. You are down to your last dime.

You peek at your hole cards to find 10♦ ♦ 9♦ ♦ and decide to limp in for a nickel. Grandma shoots you a suspicious look and taps the table, apparently having decided not to raise you from the blind this time. There are ten cents in the pot.

The flop comes 7♦ ♦ 6♠ ♠ 2♦ ♦.

Grandma leans in to get a closer look at the cards, scratches under her brassiere (usually a sure sign that she's got a hand) and throws in a nickel, which is all you have left. As you look forlornly at your cards, the old lady suffers a rare moment of pity and turns her cards faceup: 8♥ ♥ 7♥ ♥.

"You don't want to call me," she warns, picking up her knitting where she left off.

The needles go clickety-clack. Do you call Grandma's pair of sevens with your last nickel, or do you fold and wait for another hand?

♥ ♦ ♣ ♠ ♥ ♦ ♣ ♠ ♥ ♦ ♣ ♠ ♥ ♦ ♣ ♠ ♥ ♦ ♣ ♠ ♥ ♦ ♣ ♠

THE ANSWER

You quickly calculate your outs:

Any diamond will give you a flush (9 outs), an 8 will give you a straight (2 more outs, as you've already accounted for the 8♦♦, and Grandma's holding the 8♦♦), and a nine or a ten will give you a better pair (6 outs, not including the 9♦♦ and 10♦♦).

That's 17 outs, which multiplied by four gives you a 68 percent chance of winning the hand. Assuming Grandma's hand doesn't improve—she's only got three 7s in the deck to help her, as any 8 will make you a straight—you're a big favorite to win!

As the pot is laying you 3-to-1 odds on your bet (meaning that you'd only have to win 1 of every 4, or 25 percent of the time, to make this a profitable call), you toss your last nickel in and turn over your hand.

You enjoy a moment of triumph when the 10♣♣ appears on the turn, giving you top pair. "How you like me now, Nana?"

To her credit, she doesn't gloat when the 7♣♣ appears on the river, giving her trips and a winning hand. "At least you got your money into the middle when you had the best of it," she says as she rakes in the pot. "In poker, that's all you can do."

4

THE HOME GAME

You've purchased your first poker book and have inhaled the contents. You're ready to play for real.

Only you start to get the sweats at the thought of facing down a table of crocodiles at your local cardroom, or jumping into an online free-for-all game against someone who calls himself "Gotta Raise."

Your best bet, so to speak, is to find a home game.

Home games vary wildly in quality. Choose one that's too weak, and you'll find yourself playing five-card draw, hoping to catch one of the twos, threes, one-eyed jacks, suicide kings, or queens looking away from the flower that the dealer, already three sheets to the wind, has selected as the wildcard. Stumble upon a game that's too tough, and you'll be risking your mortgage payment against aggressive sharps who have taken the night off from their usual $50/100 pot limit game at the local Indian casino.

The Internet has made it a lot easier to find a home game appropriate to your bankroll and level of skill—*www.homepokergames.com*, for example, allows players to advertise their regular games and tournaments, searchable by geographical area. But if you're looking to control the quality of the players—and the play itself—there's no substitute for hosting your own game.

WHO TO INVITE

You're probably familiar with the poker adage, "If you can't spot a sucker at the table, the sucker is you."

There are some merits, however, to resisting that temptation to line your table with the dumbest and drunkest louts that you've somehow managed to stay acquainted with. Dumb and drunk people will slow down your game. They can also be models of bad behavior, encouraging you to develop your own awful habits that will ultimately cost you a small fortune.

You also want to avoid supercompetitors, bullies, poor sports, or people who will otherwise scare off any non-Type-A personalities from returning to your game. Ditto on cheaters.

The best opponents will be people who share your general level of enthusiasm for the game. Don't worry if one or two of them have a bit more experience—you'll be smart enough to stay out of their way, and you might even pick up a few of their tricks in the process.

How many people should you invite? If you're trying to learn how to play poker the "right" way, you'll want to have at least six—any fewer than that, and you'll be playing **short-handed**, a condition that requires you to dramatically change your style of play (more on that later). While you can deal hold'em to as many as twenty-three players, more than nine or ten will usually result in a game that's slow, chaotic, and extremely annoying if the cards aren't flowing your way.

SETTING

A home game doesn't have to be in your house. You can host one at a cigar club, in a hotel, or in the conference room at your office. Russ Hamilton, winner of the World Series in 1994, learned how to play in a West Virginia coal mine. High-stakes pro Jennifer Harman's first home game was in the backroom of her father's bar in Reno.

If you are using your actual home, and you don't want to ding up your dining room furniture, you're going to need a poker table. Felt is nice. Felt is better than nice. Felt is perfect.

So are padded edges, which give you a place to rest your elbows and reduce the chance of severe brain damage during those times you have to bang your head against the table.

Investing in a table has the added psychological benefit of creating return players. There's something about the allure of the felt. . . . Must . . . have . . . felt . . .

If you're not ready to invest in an actual poker table yet, throwing a blanket over a dining room table makes for a reasonable if low-rent substitute.

Two decks of cards allow you to shuffle one while the other is in play. A word of advice: Use different colors. Decks that are too "samey" have a tendency to get mixed together. Having two players turn over the same king-high flush is embarrassing and could, should you find yourself in a game of Old West desperadoes, lead to unnecessary bloodshed.

THE POKER CHIP

In *The Biggest Game in Town,* A. Alvarez quotes Jules Weintraub, a.k.a. "Big Julie," a New York poker player with a gift for observation: "The guy who invented gambling was bright, but the guy who invented the chip was a genius."

If money represents some abstracted notion of value—the reward for one's labors or the ability to purchase something new—then chips are an abstraction of money, the reward for a hand well played, the ability to see another one. That's a lot of abstraction, which might explain why so many people seem to lose the ability to connect a chip to any tangible notion of value. How much harder it would be if you had to call a $5 bet, a $50 bet, a $50,000 bet with actual cash. Tossing chips into a pot is easy. Sometimes frighteningly easy.

The truth is you've got to be able to disconnect. Deciding whether or not to move all-in, at the final table of the World Series of Poker, where a mistake could cost you more than a million dollars, would be nearly impossible if one had to look at it in terms of actual buying power. They're just chips.

The first poker chips were made of wood, bone, ivory, mother-of-pearl, and probably a few other materials that would nowadays lead animal activists to set your house on fire. Sometime in the early twentieth century, people began making chips out of clay. They still do, although hard plastic and other clay composites are also popular.

If you're going to host a home game, you're going to need a set of chips. If you want to impress your guests— going on the theory that impressed guests are more likely to return—think about investing in a set of good poker chips. The sound that a good chip makes as it hits the felt, or the "clickety-clack" as it's stacked and restacked with others of its kind, can be as beautiful as any symphony.

What makes a good poker chip? In a word: *heft.* Most cardrooms use chips that weigh 11.5 grams, almost four times heaver than those cheap plastic ones that you probably grew up playing with. There's really no substitute for the feel of a clay chip, but clay composites can be almost as good.

Unless you're planning to host a tournament, you don't have to worry about too many denominations—you'll probably never need more than two colors. The exact number you'll need will vary depending on your stakes and the psychology of your players, but fifty to one hundred chips per player will generally do the trick.

Lutz Bergman, who has been running the Poker Chip Company (*www.thepokerchipcompany.com*) since 1991, says that most of his customers spend anywhere from $100 to $3,000 on a set of new chips, depending on the quantity, style, and monogramming.

COLLECTING POKER CHIPS

In 1993, a diverse group of people gathered in a convention hall at the Aladdin Casino in Las Vegas. The turnout was quite surprising, as many of them had suspected that the common interest that had brought them together—they all collected casino chips—was too eccentric to have any kind of mass appeal. "Everybody who collected chips thought they were the only ones crazy enough to do it," says chip collector Andy Hughes. "Why would people collect something that could be traded in for real cash?"

It was the first annual meeting of the Casino Chip and Gaming Token Collectors Club, formed five years earlier by a group of enthusiasts who had met at coin collecting conventions. Today the club boasts more than 2,500 members. They meet annually in Las Vegas, but stay in touch throughout the year via their Web site and a quarterly magazine.

Whereas most of us look at a chip only long enough to see how much it's worth, seasoned collectors can immediately identify the family. Virtually every serious chip in the world is made by one of five companies, each with a unique manufacturing style. Collectors can break down the chip into its component parts: the base color, the mold, the inlay, and the inserts. They can tell you if the mold has been "incused" (pressed into) or "proud of" (raised above) the chip's surface, and expound on the difference between a satin and a slick finish.

Many collectors specialize in a single style. Limited Editions, or "LE's," are chips printed in small batches for special events—one of the first and most famous was the "TWA" produced by the Sahara for the now-defunct airline's annual convention in 1968. "Illegals" are markers from illegitimate enterprises like the Floridian Casino, once operated in Miami by the infamous Al Capone. Those who collect the plastic $2.50 chips that blackjack dealers use to make change call them "snappers." Andy Hughes focuses mainly on $5 chips from casinos that have gone out of business.

Over the years, the casinos have developed a symbiotic relationship with the collectors, encouraged, no doubt, by their odd desire to hang onto chips instead of cashing them. Binion's Horseshoe first did their part around 1995 when they created limited edition "tubes" of twenty chips, each featuring a past winner of the World Series of Poker. It's a practice that continues to this day, although many collectors will tell you that Binion's made a mistake when, after Chris Ferguson's victory in 2000, they switched from the clay chips produced by Paul-Son to the hard plastic models manufactured by Bud Jones.

Like any other collectible, certain chips achieve

value that far transcends the original denomination. Not too long ago an Ohio man browsing his
local flea market found a $5 chip from the old
Hacienda Casino. Figuring it was worth something, he posted it on eBay. The chip, which turned
out to be the only one known to still exist, sold for
more than $15,000.

———————

Chips provide an outlet for boredom as well: the chip
trick. The basic riffle (see below) is a good place to start.
Chip magicians who have achieved a certain degree of
skill can deftly shuffle a stack using only their fingers, run
a solitary chip along the back of their hands or bounce
one on the table with enough torque to make it return to
the top of their stack. Antonio Esfandiari—who on top of
being one of the best no-limit hold'em players around
happens to be, in the more traditional sense of the word, a
real magician—can pull off a few feats with his chips that
need to be seen to be believed.

———————

THE $18,000 RIFFLE

The first chip trick most players learn is the riffle.
Grab six chips from your stack and set them down

on the table. With one hand, break them into two stacks of three. Push the two stacks together, gently, while pulling them upward. After a bit of practice, two stacks will shuffle together neatly, like a deck of cards, re-forming into a single stack. Soon you'll be grabbing the six chips from your stack without even looking. Experienced rifflers can shuffle stacks of two or three times that size.

I once sat across the table from a player who recounted a cautionary tale. After teaching himself the basic riffle, he attempted to impress his father with a demonstration of his newfound dexterity. "That's great," observed his dad, in a tone that conveyed something short of enthusiasm. "How much did *that* cost you to learn?"

To which Junior was reluctantly forced to confess, "About $18,000."

You may want to consider practicing your riffling skills on your own time, saving your focus for the game in front of you.

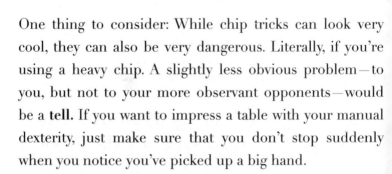

One thing to consider: While chip tricks can look very cool, they can also be very dangerous. Literally, if you're using a heavy chip. A slightly less obvious problem—to you, but not to your more observant opponents—would be a **tell.** If you want to impress a table with your manual dexterity, just make sure that you don't stop suddenly when you notice you've picked up a big hand.

In fact, the way an opponent handles chips can tell you a lot about his or her playing style. A quick glance at one's chips usually means a bet is on the way. Players who stack their chips into elaborate pyramids or other miraculous feats of architecture are people you should watch out for—holding onto one's chips long enough to engage in this kind of construction is the sign of a very patient player who isn't mixing it up in too many pots.

CARO'S BOOK OF POKER TELLS
by Mike Caro

"Players often stack chips in a manner directly indicative of their style of play. Conservative means conservative; sloppy means sloppy."

This is the first Law of Tells, according to Mike Caro, yet another alum from the team that brought you *Super/System*. The man known as "the Mad Genius of Poker" offers twenty-five in all, complete with almost two hundred photos of players engaging in all sorts of bad poker behavior.

The fact that these photos haven't been updated since the 1970s doesn't make the accompanying lessons any less relevant. (In fact, it gives the book a kind of charm that's rare among poker publications.) In nearly every game you sit down to, you'll encounter players with strong hands acting weak, with weak hands acting strong, or otherwise aligning themselves to one (or more) of the telling behaviors Caro puts forth.

A few of the most common tells will be addressed in Chapter Eight.

HOW MUCH TO PLAY FOR

Conventional wisdom dictates that a poker player should be prepared to lose about 30 big bets over the course of a typical session; that is, you might lose $120 in a $2/4 game. If your friends (or just you) are new to the game, you'll want to increase that estimate to 35 or 40 big bets.

Choosing the limits might be the most political decision you'll have to make as a host. Set the stakes too high, and you'll gradually starve players out of the game. Set them too low, and you'll have a frenzy of raising and re-raising with all kinds of junk hands, turning your purported game of skill into bingo night on steroids.

You know you're playing for the right amount when the losses sting, but don't send your players into fits of panic over exactly how their firstborn is going to attend college.

ALCOHOL

There's a really good reason why Las Vegas casinos offer free alcohol to their players: Those drinks aren't really free. Alcohol generally impairs judgment and inspires recklessness, a double whammy when you're making critical decisions about your money.*

Most top poker players avoid drinking while they play—unless there's an angle to be exploited. "If there's a pigeon who only starts drinking if someone else starts drinking," confesses Antonio Esfandiari, "I'll start drinking with them. And as they get drunk . . ."

That being said, you should probably serve drinks at your home game, or at least create an atmosphere conducive to letting loose. You might even find that a drink or two will improve your own game, as poker is a game that requires fearlessness. The trick is to find that balance between winning bravado and complete idiocy. As T. J. Cloutier once said of his old friend Bill Smith:

> "He was one of the greatest players of all time . . . the tightest player you'd ever played in your life when he was sober. And when he was halfway drunk, he was the best player I'd ever played with. But when he got past that halfway mark, he was the worst player I'd ever played with."

THE ONE-HOUR RULE

Big-time poker can often be a test of endurance—witness the World Series—but there's no reason your home game has to be. Especially if you're holding it on a weeknight.

* Drugs fall into the same basic category. Face it: Were it legal, the casinos would gladly be handing out large spliffs and other quality Colombian products to their treasured customers.

Games that run into the wee hours, along with the angry poker widows and aggravated employers they create, can turn your regulars into no-shows.

Don't let your game break up too early, either. There's nothing worse than a player who, after winning a huge pot, rises from the table to call it a night.

Agreeing in advance to an ending time helps but may put an artificial end to a game that, after hours of frustration, is just starting to get good. Another equally effective approach is the "One-Hour Rule": Tell your players that they have to announce their departure time an hour before they're planning to go. It not only saves a lot of aggravation, but can lead to a pretty exciting final hour of desperate play.

♥ ♦ ♣ ♠ ♥ ♦ ♣ ♠ ♥ ♦ ♣ ♠ ♥ ♦ ♣ ♠ ♥ ♦ ♣ ♠ ♥ ♦ ♣ ♠ ♥ ♦ ♣ ♠

YOUR DEFINING MOMENT

It's Wednesday night, a night you've come to call "The Best Night of the Week." Your friends arrive, the pizza's been ordered, and the chips have been purchased. The cards are finally in the air. You've doubled the stakes because you're all taking a road trip to Vegas next week to play **satellites** into the World Poker Tour Championship. Someone—you—needs to win enough for the buy-in, about $225.

You take your seat, strategically sitting to the left of the most aggressive (and crazy) player, Dave. You'll have great opportunities tonight to use your position to re-raise his ass and isolate him. The satellite entry fee is as good as yours.

You make a little progress in the first hour, but for some reason, Dave is playing very tight. Then it dawns on you: Dave isn't drinking.

"Hey, Dave, wanna beer?" you ask.

"You don't have any, numbnuts," he retorts, as he folds his fifteenth hand in a row. "Can't find a drop of alcohol in the entire place." You quickly fold your hand and sprint to the kitchen in search of a little action-increasing potion for your buddy.

No beer, but in a hidden cabinet, you find:

1. A half bottle of Crème de Menthe
2. A quarter bottle of very cheap rum
3. Some peppermint schnapps
4. A nearly empty bottle of Goldschlager

The meager refrigerator offers two bottles of Peach Snapple. You've already missed one hand and they are yelling for you. What do you do? Hurry—your satellite entry is at stake!

And supposing that you can mix something remotely potable, returning your game to its normal—wild—state, which of the following hands should you play from the button? Assume that five players will get involved in nearly every pot, capping the betting before the flop.

A♦3♦   10♣10♦   A♣9♦   8♦7♦   9♠6♣

J♥10♥   K♥Q♥   10♣7♣   A♣2♥   A♣J♦

K♠3♠   3♣3♦   5♥4♥   Q♥8♥   7♣7♥

♥ ♦ ♣ ♠ ♥ ♦ ♣ ♣ ♥ ♦ ♣ ♠ ♥ ♦ ♣ ♠ ♥ ♦ ♣ ♠ ♥ ♦ ♣ ♠ ♥ ♦ ♣ ♠

THE ANSWER

Get out that 32-ounce "Big Gulp" cup, pour in both bottles of Peach Snapple, the rest of the Goldschlager, and
then add as much rum as the cup will hold. A few ice
cubes should make Dave feel very special. Now, get back
to the table.

In a wild game with capped pots contested by many
players, you'll usually have to make a very strong hand—
three of a kind or better—in order to win. Given the size
of the investment you'll have to make each time you play,
the best hands are the ones that offer multiple possibilities toward that end.

A♦ 3♦ : Playable. You're not expecting a pair of aces
to hold up, but there are excellent flush and straight possibilities.

10♣ 10♦ : Playable. You're hoping to flop a set or an
overpair to the board.

A♣ 9♦ : Get rid of it. A trouble hand won't make a
BIG hand unless you manage to make a full house.

8♦ 7♦ : Playable. Easy to play—if you don't flop a
great hand (or draw), you're done with it.

9♣ 6♣ : Get rid of it. Don't get lured into playing
"Big Lick"—two-card gaps are hard to fill.

J♥ 10♠ : Get rid of it. Normally a solid hand, but not
worth the big investment here.

K♥ Q♥ : Playable. This is a very good hand for a multiway capped pot.

10♣ 7♦ : Get rid of it. Even if the flop miraculously
fills your gap, anyone with a J-10 is on a better straight
draw than you.

A♣ 2♥ : Get rid of it. No weak aces in this game
unless they're suited!

A♣ J♦ : Playable. Only barely, due to the high card
strength.

K♠ 3♠ : Get rid of it. Even though it's suited, this is a
trouble hand. There are too many ways you can connect
with the board but still wind up second best.

3♣ 3♦ : Get rid of it. Playing small pocket pairs in
pots like this is suicide.

5♥ 4♥ : Flip a coin. Nice straight possibilities, but if
you flop the flush, you're going to be living in fear of a
fourth heart on the turn or river.

Q♥ 8♥ : Get rid of it. Decent flush potential, but it's
very difficult to fill in a three-gap straight.

7♣ 7♠ : Another coin flip. This is about the cutoff
under these conditions—bigger pairs are definitely
playable, smaller ones can be tossed away.

5

HOW TO THINK LIKE A POKER PLAYER

Poker players are a wily breed. Like there's any choice. While the fluctuations of Lady Luck can make Vanderbilts out of madmen and turn sane, responsible players into broken, wrecked vestiges of humanity, the truth is that over the long haul, only the strong survive.

Which raises the question, what makes a strong poker player? Is it cleverness, or daring? A razor-sharp mathematical mind, or a deep understanding of human psychology?

It's safe to say that all of these qualities in some way or another contribute to the makeup of a top-notch player. But perhaps more important than any of these individual traits is something that we'll call the poker mind-set. That is, how to think like a poker player.

WHY DO WE PLAY?

In my younger and more vulnerable years my father gave me some advice that I've been turning over in my mind ever since. "Whenever you feel like criticizing anyone," he told me, "just remember that all the people in the world haven't had the advantages that you've had."

— F. SCOTT FITZGERALD, *The Great Gatsby*

You're sitting in a low-limit hold'em game. It's late, you're **stuck,** and you haven't seen a playable hand in what seems like hours. Meanwhile, the guy across the table from you—let's call him "the Drunk"—is playing every hand he's dealt and is winning way more than his fair share of them, knocking down another beer with each large pot that he rakes in.

A new deal. Several players limp in before you, on the button, look down to find a suited ace-king. You raise, the blinds fold, the limpers all call, building a nice little pot.

The flop comes A-9-4 **rainbow.** So far, so good. Everyone checks to you. You bet, leading all of your opponents to fold. That is, except for the Drunk, who obviously hasn't paid a lick of attention to the tight **table image** (more on what this is below) you've been maintaining all night. "What the heck!" he says as he calls.

The turn card brings a beautiful king, giving you top two pair. The Drunk checks to you, and you bet. He takes a swig of his beer, tosses in enough chips to call, and gazes to the heavens. "Gimme a deuce!" he yells.

The dealer lays down the river card. Sure enough, it's a deuce. The Drunk slaps the table, lets out a laugh of unrestrained joy, and throws in a bet. Every instinct tells you that, somehow, he has you beat, but you make the crying call.

He flips over pocket deuces—giving him a set over your two pair—and starts piling the chips, *your chips*. Your vision starts to get hazy. How could he have called you? He only had two outs!

Experienced players will recognize this tale as a classic bad beat story. You were a 22-to-1 favorite (96 percent) going into the river! How, you might ask yourself, could the Drunk have been such an idiot as to call?

Setting aside for a moment any issue of the Drunk's intelligence, a better question to ask might be, "What are the psychological factors that contributed to the Drunk's decision to chase such an improbable **suckout**?"

Everyone has a different set of reasons for playing poker. Some players enjoy the social interaction. Others enjoy the contest of wills, the chance to prove that he or she is smarter, braver, or sneakier than everyone else at the table. A good many of the players you'll face (especially at the lower limits) love to gamble, thriving on the feeling that fate, luck, destiny, and/or the spiritual being of choice is shining some divine light on them, if only for a fleeting moment.

A winning poker player recognizes—and takes advantage of—the motivations that drive others to play the game. The *social butterflies* like to be liked, are often reluctant to bluff, and are prone to showing you when they've got the goods (thus saving you a bet on the end). The *ego-*

tists can be led into making mistakes, overplaying some hands while costing themselves bets in an effort to make fancy plays that prove how clever they are. As for the *gamblers*, well, luck eventually runs out . . . hopefully, before they've taken all of your money.

These types of players face a huge disadvantage when they encounter a poker player who is motivated by one unwavering goal: *to win money.* This isn't to say that you shouldn't be social, make fancy plays, or take some chances, as long as you're doing it to win more money.

Good poker players rarely criticize their opponent's play—you don't want to scare suckers from the table, or even worse, motivate them to start playing better. Think of it this way: When you're at a pet store, there is almost always a sign that says: DON'T TAP ON THE AQUARIUM.

The best players know how to "train" their adversaries. Raising before the flop with a junk hand (which you later show down, hopefully as you're raking in the chips) is a good way to get your opponents to pay you off those times you're holding a legitimate hand. Another example is to "always" play a hand a certain way—for example, consistently raising with a draw to a flush—then suddenly doing the opposite. The goal is not only to keep your opponents off-balance, but to keep them off-balance in a predictable way.

Of course, your more skilled opponents will not only know that you are trying to train them, but will be trying their hardest to do the same to you.

WHAT KIND OF PLAYER ARE YOU?

Poker games—and the people who play them—
can generally be described with two sets of
competing adjectives: loose or tight, passive or
aggressive.

A **loose** player plays a lot of different starting
hands, often disregarding strategic considerations
like position or the raise in front of them. A **tight**
player, in contrast, plays very few hands, waiting
patiently for what seem to be the most opportune
moments to enter a pot. By extension, a loose
game features a lot of players in every pot, while
in a tight game, each hand is generally contested
by only two or three players.

A **passive** player tends to check and call, usually
content to let others take the lead unless he or she
has the absolute nuts. **Aggressive** players are proponents of the "raise or fold" philosophy of poker,
the virtues of which are expounded upon later in
this chapter. A passive game offers a lot of checking and calling, while an aggressive game boasts
more raising and re-raising.

Most newcomers start out as loose and passive.
Poker veterans will sometimes refer to this type of
player as a **calling station** or an ATM (as in "**cash
machine**").

You'll encounter many players who like to play

loose and aggressive. They are the gamblers, bluffing frequently and occasionally winning with all kinds of **junk** hands. They also tend to go broke. (On your bad days, however, these types of players demonstrate a most unpleasant tendency to break *you* in the process.)

Tight-passive players are often called **rocks,** as it's about as easy to win money from them, so the expression goes, as it is to draw blood from a stone. The good news is that you really have to bend over backward to lose money to this type of player: When a rock bets, he or she can be counted on to have the goods.

Most poker players strive to be tight and aggressive. They choose their battles carefully, looking for those situations where they have the best of it. Once engaged in battle, they are tenacious fighters, raising and re-raising with ferocious (but controlled) aggression.

There are exceptions to this rule. Gus Hansen, for one, is a player who has had a lot of success with a loose-aggressive style. It's a difficult style to play well, but can be even more difficult to defend against. This may sound counterintuitive, but as your level of skill increases, you can actually begin to play more hands before the flop, as your decision-making will be superior to your opponents. You'll extract extra bets on the hands you win, and escape cheaply those times you run into trouble.

Don't fall into the common trap of overestimating

your poker skills—you're not Gus Hansen yet. Playing tight-aggressive poker is a winning strategy and the one you should employ.

EVERYTHING IS ZEN

It's just a job. Grass grows, birds fly, waves pound the sand. I just beat people up.

—MUHAMMAD ALI

There's a poker adage that goes something like, "If you can't play with a smile, then don't play at all."

Whoever originally said this obviously was miraculously enlightened, utterly insane, or benefiting from some very effective medication. No one can play happy all of the time. There will be hands, sessions, weeks—even months—when the luck of the cards seems to be running against you. When every maniac seemingly intent on losing his or her bankroll to your solid, steady play manages to hit that miracle card (or, when things are really bad, two running cards) to crack your pocket aces.

The great poker players know that bad beats are an inevitable part of the game. Examined from a slightly different angle, *most* of your beats should be bad beats, as you're generally pouring money into the pot in those situations when you already have the best of it, or at least have the right pot odds to hang around for a draw. What's more, you should *want* your opponents to play badly. Yes, it sucks when someone hits a 22-to-1 long shot against you. Over the long haul, however, you should be pocketing his or her desperate money the other 21 times.

Experienced poker players know this, and most have learned to combat any feelings of despair with a Zen-like consciousness. Hands come, hands go. You just play poker.

Not unlike the mastery of Zen, this kind of inner peace comes only with practice. When asked what it feels like to lose $100,000 in a single session, Jennifer Harman offered this reply:

> "You don't even think about it. But, you know, it's hard getting to this frame of mind, believe me. . . . The first time I lost $3,000, I went home and cried like a baby. . . . When I lost $10,000, same thing. When I lost $30,000, I couldn't sleep for four days. When I lost $100,000, for the first time in my life, I couldn't sleep for a week. But then, the next time I lost $100,000, and the next time I lost $100,000, you know, it's like your pain threshold just goes up."

This "letting go" isn't just applied to losing sessions, but to individual hands as well. One of the hardest concepts for a new player to grasp is the idea that once you've thrown your chips into the center of the table, your connection to them has ended. Regardless of how much a professional player has personally "invested" in any particular pot, he or she will continue to make or call bets only as long as the odds of winning the pot justify further investment. Laying down a once-powerful hand in the face of overwhelming evidence that it's become second-best is a sign of a good poker player.

Keep the acronym H.A.L.T. near the top of your mind. If you are Hungry, Angry, Lonely, or Tired, you shouldn't be at the table. As poker author John Fox once wrote, "The best player in the world with a temporarily dulled brain is not even a match for an average player using full concentration." Save yourself the embarrassment of blowing your bankroll in a less-than-tip-top state of mind—simply HALT.

ZEN AND THE ART OF POKER
by Larry W. Phillips

This journey to poker enlightenment starts with a quote from *Caddyshack*, "Be the ball," perhaps fooling you into believing that the information you are holding in your hands is at best humorous, at worst trivial. It's both, of course, which is what makes this little book so powerful.

Phillips, a writer, journalist, and longtime poker player, uses quotes from Sun Tzu to Chuck Norris to illuminate one hundred truths about the game, from "Learn to use inaction as a weapon" to "Make sure you know when you're on a cold streak." An entertaining read, to be sure, but also a deceptively insightful lesson in developing a poker mind-set.

GAME SELECTION

I don't care to belong to any club that will have me as a member.

— GROUCHO MARX

Imagine being the ninth best poker player in the world. It would feel pretty good, right? Sure it would, unless you're sitting at a table with the eight players who are better than you. Perhaps the most important decision a poker player has to make is whether or not to sit down at a particular game.

First, you need to consider your opposition. As the cliché goes, if you can't spot the fish, it's probably you. Make sure that there is at least one person who is stupid, exhausted, desperate, irrational, and/or drunk enough for you to outplay.

You also have to compare the tone of the game with your personal style of play. If you are someone who just *loves* to bluff, you're not going to do very well in a game of loose, passive players who will call you all the way to a showdown. If you are a patient, calculating sort, you're going to do best against those Type As who will raise your nut hands on the final street.

Remember that you'll likely make a lot more money in a lower stakes game that you can run over than you will in a higher stakes game where you have to fight for every chip.

Almost as important as selecting the right game is choosing the best seat. A game that is eminently beatable from one side of the table may be tragically unprofitable if you find yourself in the wrong chair. This isn't about superstition—despite what you'll often hear from your fellow players, there's no such thing as a "cold" seat—but about position, which you've already discovered to be one of the most important aspects of the game.

You generally want the hyperaggressive players on your right and the tight-ass rocks on your left. When the maniac comes into the pot, you will re-raise and "isolate" him from the tight-ass rocks, who will likely fold to your double-sized bet. You'll play for pots heads-up, in superior position, and—assuming you're not a maniac yourself when it comes to hand selection—usually with a hand that's a favorite to win.

Now look at what would happen were the situation reversed, with the tight rocks on your right and the maniac on your left. Every time you enter the pot, the maniac raises or re-raises, while the rocks—who are no strangers to the isolation strategy—won't be afraid to re-raise. Now it's *you* who will be facing a double raise, often out of position. Change your seat, even if it means getting up from the game!

Any time there are multiple open seats at a table when you arrive, take a few minutes to figure out which will be the most profitable. Your win rate depends on it.

BANKROLL

When I have to put my money out there, my money's out there. Everybody knows that. . . . So if you want to mess with me, it's going to cost you. . . . You have to be willing to die in order to live in these tournaments. . . . That's basically it.

—AMIR VAHEDI, *ESPN's 2003 World Series of Poker*

This philosophy, which has served Vahedi so well—he's one of the world's best no-limit hold'em players—applies to any and all levels of play. A poker player should be always be concentrating on winning, and never *not losing*. "Scared money" rarely wins, especially against aggressive players who are able to recognize it. Poker is a game of critical decisions. It's not easy to make these decisions when their outcome could affect your ability to pay the rent or put dinner on the table.

As Chip Reese once said of a fellow Poker Hall of Famer: "If you think about what money can do for you, you're gone. That's what made Stuey Ungar such a great no-limit player: He never, ever, *ever* cared."*

A good rule of thumb is this: If you can't say to yourself "they're only chips" as you fling a bet into the pot, then you are probably playing in a game beyond your means.

As we've mentioned previously, conventional wisdom suggests that you should be willing to lose (and thus ready to play) twenty times more than the maximum bet. However, there's more to choosing a limit than just bankroll. Limit games are generally divided into three basic categories, each with its own psychology (or, some might say, psychosis).

LOW-LIMIT GAMES

Low-limit games, ranging from 10¢/20¢ to $6/12, are generally populated by players who are new to the game, aren't good enough to compete for higher stakes, or are playing for the sheer fun of it. As a result, you tend to see

* Yes, there is a Poker Hall of Fame at Binion's Horseshoe, which has been inducting a new player each year since its inception in 1979.

people playing too many hands and taking them too far. Winning at the lower limits requires a great deal of patience and a strong understanding of pot odds—you're going to make most of your money by making "good" decisions (i.e., mathematically correct) while forcing your opponents to make "bad" ones. It generally doesn't make sense to do a lot of bluffing in these games, because for a bluff to be successful, you've got to be playing against people who are willing to fold. Nor is it particularly useful to make a lot of fancy plays, as your opponents are unlikely to respond to (or even notice) your artistry. Because most of the players are going to be involved in most of the pots, chasing miraculous cards, the odds are much better that one or two of them will actually make their hands, meaning that you are going to take a lot of bad beats.

Most experienced players view low-limit poker as something akin to working in a salt mine. It's hard work, occasionally painful, and—once the basic concepts are grasped—pretty damn boring. But for new players, there's no substitute for this kind of initiation. Keep in mind that a good poker player will, more times than not, utterly destroy low-limit games. If you can't win consistently at these games, don't be so quick to blame the bad beats—you probably have some more work to do before you move up.

MIDDLE-LIMIT GAMES

This term is used to describe that narrow but popular range of games between $10/20 and $80/160. Generally, you'll be facing other players who are pretty good and/or have a lot of money to lose. You'll need all of the skills that helped you to win at the lower limits — a **leak** in your game that cost you a few dollars a session in the smaller games will cost you hundreds, if not thousands, in a middle-limit contest. What really distinguishes this game, however, is the emphasis on bankroll and the ability to wield it aggressively. From a psychological standpoint, it's quite a different experience to toss in a $60 bet than one for $6, and losing $3,000 feels a lot worse than losing $300. Your opponents know this, and will repeatedly "put you to the test," raising and re-raising with marginal hands or draws to see if you have the guts to call or, more importantly, throw in your own raises and re-raises. You need to approach a middle-limit game with a bankroll that can withstand these attacks and allow you to play with fear-lessness.

HIGH-LIMIT GAMES

These are the games where legends are made while small fortunes are routinely exchanged. The term "high-limit" is used to describe games from $100/200 on up, but as you might guess, the difference in average pot size between a $200/400 and a $50,000/100,000 game (yes, one was recently run at the Bellagio in Las Vegas) is, in an understatement, substantial. In fact, this category is occasionally further delineated to include an "ultra-high-limit" game, but the basic principles of either are the same.

You'll of course need the same skills and fearlessness that allowed you to succeed at the lower and medium level games, but you'll have to supplement your play with a superior understanding of human psychology.

High-limit poker is a game of psychological levels. At the most basic level, there's the hand you have, and the hand you think your opponent has. Ratchet this up a notch, and start to consider the hand your opponent thinks that you have, and the hand that your opponent thinks that you think he or she has. It's possible to take this kind of thinking to even higher levels. In short, certain plays that would seem absolutely idiotic at one level of thinking might be considered sublime masterpieces of deception when examined through the filter of a higher level.

The trick, of course, is determining which level of thinking your opponent is using (and, in turn, the level your opponent *wants* you to believe that he or she is using.) As you might guess, the result can often be a labyrinthine battle of wits to make your head explode. Many top players are thus adherents of **game theory,** the branch of mathematics devoted to the study of really, really complex decision-making. In its most sophisticated practice, game theorists will make certain decisions *totally at random* in order to confuse their opponents.

Take a minute to let that sink in: You're wagering thousands, even millions, of dollars on the basis of completely random decisions. This is high-limit poker.

THE VIRTUE OF AGGRESSION

Check, check, check, chicken!
　　　　　　　　　　— A COMMON POKER TAUNT

If there is one "X-factor" that unites all great poker players, it's their willingness to play aggressive poker.

Like it or not, aggression seems to have a magical effect at most poker tables. A strong raise is usually better than a mere call, and when you can't raise, folding should at least be seriously considered.

There are many reasons why aggression is such a force to be reckoned with. Here are a few:

Aggression forces your opponents to react.

Nobody likes to make tough decisions. When you are able to take control of the betting, you make the other guy guess, worry, and, when things are going your way, lay down a better hand than yours.

Aggression lets you know where you stand.

While it's not always the most cost-efficient way of acquiring information from your opponents, it is usually the most effective. A player who calls your raise is often on a draw, or has a made hand that he or she is not so confident about. An opponent's re-raise or check-raise should be acknowledged as a sign of strength, usually denoting a powerful made hand or an excellent draw.

Aggression gets you "free cards" and prevents you from giving them away.

As discussed in the previous chapter, a well-timed bet or raise before the flop or on an early street can let you see a card on a later, more expensive street, for free, occasionally allowing you to improve your hand. The opposite is also true—it's generally an error of the worst kind to allow your opponent to see a free card when you have the best hand.

Aggression can turn a second-best hand into a drawing hand.

Here's an example: In a $6/12 Texas Hold'em game, an early position player comes in for a raise. A player in middle position calls the $12 bet. Everyone else folds to you in the small blind, where you discover pocket queens and decide to re-raise to $18. The big blind calls, as do the other two players, creating a $72 pot.

The flop comes A-K-10, far from ideal for your queens. You bet, the big blind calls, the original raiser *raises*, causing the player in middle position to fold.

You're pretty sure at this point that you have the second best hand, as the raiser's bound to have an ace or a king, possibly even three of a kind. But should you fold? Thanks to your aggressive betting, not only do you have a pretty good idea of where you stand, but the $96 in the pot makes it correct for you to do something that your grandfather warned you never to do: draw for the inside straight. Sure, the odds against you hitting a jack on the turn are about 12-to-1, but you're getting 16-to-1 from the pot. Aggression has "magically" transformed your hand into a worthwhile draw.

THE INNER VOICE

I felt a great disturbance in the Force.
—SIR ALEC GUINNESS AS BEN "OBI-WAN" KENOBI,
Star Wars

All of the great poker players have it: an inner voice. It tells them when their opponent is weak, and it can be moved off a hand with a well-timed bluff. Or it acts as an alarm bell, signaling darker menace in what, on the surface, seemed to be an innocuous call.

Some call it ESP. Others attribute it to some preternatural awareness of fear, hormones, or vibrational energy. Rationalists will claim that the ability to "sense" that something is wrong is just the ability, acquired with years of experience, to recognize a subtle inconsistency in the way things should normally play out.

Whatever it is, you need to learn it. Once you've learned to hear this inner voice, you're ready to embark on the even greater challenge of listening to it.

THERE'S NO "ALWAYS" IN POKER

A foolish consistency is the hobgoblin of little minds.
— RALPH WALDO EMERSON

Contrary to what some books (and even more players) will tell you, the only "right" way to play poker is the way that consistently wins you money.

Even if that means being inconsistent.

♥ ♦ ♣ ♠ ♥ ♦ ♣ ♠ ♥ ♦ ♣ ♠ ♥ ♦ ♣ ♠ ♥ ♦ ♣ ♠ ♥ ♦ ♣ ♠

YOUR DEFINING MOMENT

You've arrived about two hours late to a $10/20 home game hosted by your golf pro. Five players are seated at a small table, and to your surprise there are no empty chairs.

"Glad you could make it!" says the Pro. "Five-hundred-dollar buy-in, if you can handle it. My kid will grab an extra chair from upstairs . . . we'll make room for you."

You have about five minutes to decide where you want the chair to go. Being the aspiring professional that you are, you study the table, the action, and the players in between bites of cracker with cheese dip.

Seat 1: The Pro. $500 in chips. He's drinking Budweiser.

Seat 2: The Cartboy. $200. Coke.

Seat 3: The Greenskeeper. $650. Clear liquid.

Seat 4: The Caddy: $800. Clear liquid w/a slice of lime.

Seat 5: The Bartender. $350. Something in a martini glass.

The Pro is on the button, the small and big blinds are posted by the Cartboy and the Greenskeeper respectively. You stand behind the Greenskeeper, who lets you peek at his cards—an ace-ten offsuit. The Caddy takes a swig of his drink—"Raise it up, boys, I'm in a rush!" and tosses $20 into the pot. The Bartender and the Pro both call. The Cartboy folds, accidentally exposing his K♣ 10♠ . The Greenskeeper thinks for a bit but finally folds his hand.

Three-way action.

The flop comes A♦ 9♦ 3♦ . The Caddy tosses in a $10 bet. The Bartender shakes his head and calls. The Pro calls quickly, which you know from past experience usually indicates he's on a draw.

The turn is the 10♦ . The Caddy checks, the Bartender checks, and the Pro stews for a bit and finally checks.

The river brings the J♠ . The Caddy quickly fires a bet. "Twenty dollars, boys, twenty dollars." The Bartender calls, as does the pro. It's a showdown.

The board: A♦ 9♦ ♦ 3♦ ♦ 10♦ ♦ J♣

The Caddy shows J♣ 7♦ ♦ for a flush.

The Bartender shows J♦ 9♠ ♠ for a slightly better flush.

The Pro opens his A♠ Q♦ , a queen-high flush and the best hand. "Damn," he exclaims as he rakes in the chips. I was afraid that one of you had the king of diamonds."

Pro Jr. arrives with your chair. "Make some room for the new blood!" Where do you ask him to put it?

♥ ♦ ♣ ♠ ♥ ♦ ♣ ♠ ♥ ♦ ♣ ♠ ♥ ♦ ♣ ♠ ♥ ♦ ♣ ♠ ♥ ♦ ♣ ♠

THE ANSWER

You don't have a lot of information about these players, but you have enough to make an educated guess. You recall the mantra, "Maniacs on your right, tight asses on your left."

Clearly the Caddy—who just raised under the gun with jack-seven offsuit—and the Bartender—who called his raise with an unsuited 10-9—are the maniacs of the bunch. The Pro is not only playing squeaky tight, but weak as well, failing to bet or raise with what turned out to be the strongest hand throughout. The Greenskeeper and the Cartboy both threw away playable hands in the face of a raise, signaling tight, tight, tight.

You slide up your chair between the Bartender and the Pro and pop open a beer (just to seem social). You look down at your first hand and find two aces—"pocket rockets." It's looking like your mom will be getting a very, very nice present for Mother's Day.

6

ONLINE POKER

It's 8:30 A.M. You crawl out of bed, pull on your bathrobe. Coffee. You run a hand through your hair and power up the computer. Two minutes later, you are engaged in an all-out raising war with some businessman on his lunch break . . . in Tokyo.

Online poker has revolutionized the way poker is played. It's brought the game to an international cast of rounders, many of whom live hundreds of miles from the nearest casino. The online cardrooms have created a magical poker wonderland where there's action, somewhere in the world, twenty-four/seven. Mothers send their kids to school with a kiss, before check-raising a full house on the river for a pot that will cover lunch money for the next six months. Mild-mannered accountants use their lunch break to bluff aggressively at pots that won't pay for a cup of coffee. A grandmother in Saginaw proves that she can curse like a sailor after taking a bad beat from a Finnish guy who calls himself "PhilHellmuth95."

There are complete novices. There are professionals—a growing number—who make a living off the ready availability of loose games, sometimes playing two (or more) at the same time.

Online poker lacks the charm of a live game. Conversation is limited. The sound effects get monotonous. You can't play with your chips.

Then again, you can play in your bathrobe—or without it.

STAKING A CLAIM

In theory, choosing a place to play couldn't be simpler. You want to go someplace that delivers the game you want, with the action you're looking for, at the times you want to play. You want that place to be reputable and to pay cashouts in a timely fashion.

There's no governing body that regulates online poker sites, as most of them are located offshore. This makes some people uneasy. If you are a poker player, you are probably not one of these people.

Doing a little research beforehand can save some heartache. There's probably no reason for saying this other than gut instinct, but sites affiliated with professional poker players are probably going to do their best to stay reputable—in this media-saturated world, no professional wants egg on his or her face.

FULL TILT POKER
WWW.FULLTILTPOKER.COM

Chris "Jesus" Ferguson. Howard Lederer. Phil Ivey. Erick Lindgren. John Juanda. Eric Seidel. Andy Bloch. Clonie Gowen. And last but not least, your author, Phil Gordon.

These nine players represent, as of 2004, more than twenty World Series of Poker bracelets, one world championship, no less than six wins and dozens of final table appearances on the World Poker Tour.

You can find each of us playing exclusively at FullTiltPoker.com, an online cardroom that we designed and engineered ourselves. You're cordially invited to come and watch, play against, and learn from some of the best players in the world.

PokerPulse (*www.pokerpulse.com*) lets you see, in real time, how many tables are going at most of the major online cardrooms. Check out the online poker discussion forums like RGP (short for the news server rec.gambling.poker) or 2+2 (*www.twoplustwo.com*, hosted by none other than Sklansky and Malmuth) to see what people are complaining about. Some complaints are valid. Spotty server issues are bad. So are cash withdrawals that take too long, and cheating (more on this later). Almost every site is at some time or another accused of (a) juicing its pots and increasing the size of the **rake*** with *action flops,* cards that hit a lot of players at the same time in a way that just can't be random; and (b) housing a clever computer algorithm that penalizes players foolish enough to make withdrawals from the site with long, unbelievably painful runs of losing cards. To date, neither of these claims has ever been verified, and may very well be the urban legends of the online poker world, disseminated by players unfamiliar with the laws of statistical variance.

Then again, it never hurts to be a little paranoid. If something just doesn't seem right with a site, move your money to another one. There are plenty of them out there.

Consider starting with a small deposit, making sure that the site fits your needs. If you like to play Omaha hi-lo8 before breakfast, or multi-table no-limit tournaments on Sundays, you'll want to make sure that those games are regularly populated with the kinds of players that you want to play against. Observe their vibes — do they jump around from game to game, or do they stick with the same one for hours on end? Withdraw some cash and make sure the payout gets processed fast and conveniently.

You don't have to choose just one site. Some have better tournaments, or offer **freerolls** to regular players. Others have lively short-handed games. Most offer a substantial bonus on first-time deposits, "free" money as long as you don't mind playing a minimum number of hands (and paying the rake associated with it).

Most credit card companies refuse to have anything to do

---

* The **rake** is the amount that the cardroom takes out of every pot. It's usually a couple of bucks, but some online sites charge more. The concept of *beating the rake* gets discussed in the next chapter.

with online houses of chance. Neteller (*www.neteller.com*) makes a nice alternative and interacts with almost every online site — you can make free transactions directly to and from your bank account, while earning free entries into cash lotteries. A number of "vault" sites have arisen as well, one-stop shops that let you manage your money across a network of participating sites.

CHOOSING A GAME

The "lobby" of any online site is a great source of information. Most will list the players in each game, show you the percentage of the flops that they're seeing (helping you find a loose or tight game, depending on your preference) and how many hands are being played an hour. The games with larger-than-average pots and a high percentage of people seeing the flop are going to be your most profitable.

Most sites will let you play in more than one game at the same time, which has its advantages and disadvantages.* Some players claim that multiple games force them to play a more disciplined brand of poker, not to mention allowing them to double/triple/quadruple the **hourly rate** they'd earn at just one table. It's hard to maintain a "feel" for more than one game at a time, however, which can cause you to overlook some profitable opportunities and may leave you vulnerable to bluffs, as you are less in tune with your opponents' ebbs and flows. If it seems like you are being slowed down in one game by your attention to another, players will get pissed off at you. (How you use this information is up to you.)

* Phil Ivey has been known to play in *seven* games at once. Erick "E-Dog" Lindgren claims to have played in three games simultaneously, on a cellular modem, while driving from Las Vegas to Los Angeles. Neither behavior is recommended.

PLAYING SHORT-HANDED

The lineup in an online game tends to be more fluid than a brick-and-mortar counterpart. The ease of switching tables—even sites—leads players to drop in and out of games with dizzying speed. Like it or not, at times you are going to be looking at a bunch of empty seats, playing short-handed.

There are several substantial differences between playing against nine opponents and playing against three or four. In a short-handed game, you simply have to play more hands, as you'll be required to post blinds more often than usual. Drawing hands become less valuable—there often won't be enough players contesting the pot to give you the right odds to chase your hand—while high cards and pocket pairs increase in potency, as they frequently don't need to improve to win a showdown against a limited field. As a result, there is a lot more raising before the flop with hands that you wouldn't necessarily raise with in a full game, like A-9 or 6-6.

These idiosyncrasies are even more evident against only one or two opponents. Flopping **bottom pair** in a full game is often a good reason to fold. Against a single opponent, however, it's an invitation to raise, maybe even re-raise. Ace-high is often good enough to take down a pot on the river. There are players, like Howard Lederer, who sometimes advocate raising from the button with virtually *any* hand in a heads-up confrontation, as your opponent, more often than not, will fail to connect with the flop, allowing you to use your superior position to steal more than your fair share of pots.

When you are playing short-handed, you might find it useful to imagine that you're in a full game where everyone has folded to you. In other words, if you're the first to act in a four-person game, evaluate your hand as you would were you in a full game, seated just to the right of the button, after every player before you has tossed their cards into the muck.

Keep in mind that the extra hands you're playing in a short-handed game will exacerbate any swings in your bankroll. You'll win and lose large amounts a lot more quickly than you would in a full game. Make sure that you're prepared—financially and mentally—for these radical swings before you continue playing.

In fact, you may want to avoid short-handed games altogether until you feel confident that you can outplay most of your opponents after the flop. They are, however, great practice for tournaments—you can't win a final table without playing short-handed—and can be extremely profitable.

RING GAMES VS. TOURNAMENTS

Most online cardrooms offer tournaments in addition to their regular games. Which you choose should be dictated by what aspects of your game you are trying to work on.

Most online tournaments use rapidly escalating blind structures, sometimes increasing the limits after every ten hands played. (In contrast, the blinds at the World Series of Poker are increased every two hours.) Let's say you start with $1,000 in chips. This may be plenty of ammunition when the blinds are at $5/10, but fifty hands later, when the blinds have increased to $50/100, a bad decision—or an unlucky river card—can wipe out your entire stack.

It's not uncommon to go fifty hands without winning a pot. Patience—an absolutely critical quality to being a great poker player—is a luxury that you won't have in most online tournaments. You are going to have to gamble a lot more than usual in order to win.

Impatient gambling is exactly what you *don't* want to do if you're just beginning your poker education. You're probably better off, therefore, beginning with those crazy ring games, where you can learn to throw away hand after hand until you develop a better understanding of how to value your cards in relation to any given situation.

That's not to say online tournaments aren't incredibly valuable. We'll talk a lot more about them in Chapter Ten.

SETTING

A good poker player is always observing his or her opponents, identifying betting patterns (something you should be doing as you play online) and looking for physical tells (something you can't). There's not a lot to look at in a virtual cardroom, and you'll occasionally be tempted to talk on the phone, watch TV, or surf the Web for more engaging eye candy.

Be aware of not being aware. If you're going to play serious online poker, create an environment around you that best allows you to focus on the game.

A NOTE ON "SQUIRRELING"

When you "sit down" at an online table, there's generally a default minimum you'll be required to pony up in order to play.

Some players like to start with the minimum, figuring it limits the amount they can lose. Plus, goes the reasoning, when they are forced to go all-in—that is, pushing the last of their chips into the middle—they get to see any remaining cards without having to call any more bets.

This reasoning becomes so seductive to some players that they start to "squirrel away" their money, periodically pulling chunks of it off the table in order to minimize the amount of money they have in play. You aren't allowed to do this in a brick-and-mortar cardroom, but online there's nothing to prevent you from quickly exiting a table with your money, then sitting down in the same seat with the minimum buy-in.

The problem with this strategy, at least for a good poker player, is that it costs you money. If you're only making and calling bets with positive expectations, then, by keeping yourself short of chips, you are actually reducing the amount that you will win. Sure, by going all-in you may get to see a card or two for free that could make you a big hand, but you lose out on the extra money that you'd make during the betting on those later, more expensive streets.

A corollary to this strategy is the "hit and run," where a player will hang around until he or she wins a big pot, then quickly move to another table (or log off entirely). This tactic is a loser for the same reason—while you might be limiting the amount you can lose, you are certainly limiting the amount you can win. You may be hurting yourself even more by failing to take advantage of your table image—it's a lot easier to separate opponents from their money when they think you're on a winning streak.

The simple point is this: If you are a poker player who consistently makes decisions that carry a positive expectation, then placing artificial limits on your play will, in the long run, cost you money.

YOUR FELLOW PLAYERS

The obvious downside of online play is the inability to see the people whom you are playing against. You don't know if they flinched as they called a bet, or if the vein in their neck is pulsing faster than it was a second ago.

That's not to say that there isn't any information to be gleaned from them. The name a person chooses says something about his or her personality. A guy whose name is GottaRaise! is likely to play differently than BettysGrandmother. Bluffer666 is probably fun to play against. Or not: Many online handles are double-entendres, or triple-entendres, chosen to make you misconstrue the namesake's true personality. HotBlonde69, in all likelihood, is neither hot, blonde, nor especially flexible.

If you're observant, you might be able to pick up some online tells. Players who seem to hesitate before a bet may be calculating the pot odds to a draw. (They might also be *pretending* to calculate the odds to a draw. Or, in other cases, just suffering from a bad Internet connection.) Most sites allow players to preselect a call, raise, or fold by checking a box, increasing the speed of the game, but giving away valuable information about his or her decision-making process.

It's a lot easier for most players to click a mouse than to toss chips into a physical pot. Players who make their decisions very quickly can often be exploited.

A lot of players also hit the wrong button by accident, especially if they're playing in multiple games (another valuable piece of information to obtain). So if a raise seems too out of the blue, well, it's something to consider, anyway. Hitting the wrong button yourself isn't such a bad thing to do from time to time: It mixes up your table image and will occasionally deliver a tilt-inducing bad beat.

Many sites allow you to keep notes on your opponents, as well as to track your own statistics, like the percentage of the flops you're seeing or how often you merely call a bet, an especially useful feature if you're looking for leaks in your game.

HAND HISTORY

Nearly all online sites allow you the ability to download a history of every hand that you have played. These histories include the names of each of the players, their respective stack sizes and actions on each street, and the details of any cards that are exposed in a showdown. They can be extremely valuable in your education and in improving your game. If, during the course of play, you feel like you could have played a hand in a different (or better) way, download the hand history, save it, and review it later. Better yet, share it with a "poker mentor" who can offer a constructive critique of your play.

THE CHAT BOX

The other conduit of information is, of course, the chat box. Some players are chatterboxes, usually indicating a deep need to be liked. Others avoid all conversation, conveying a total seriousness about the business at hand. Players who like to criticize the play of you or anyone else tend to be emotional players who can be put on tilt. Drunk players usually don't type very well.

Someday soon, linguistic scientists will officially declare the stuff that goes on in chat boxes to be the new universal language, succeeding where Esperanto failed. Type in **nh, ty,** or **rotflmao,** and you'll be clearly understood by people from every corner of the earth.

:) *happy face.* When you're happy and you want them to know it.
:(*sad face.* Because poker can be sad.

brb *be right back.* Usually denotes a trip to the bathroom, perhaps explaining the tight play of the last half-hour.

gg *good going.* Generally invoked right after someone's knocked out of a tournament by the relieved players who are left.

gl all *good luck all.* Few really mean it.

gtg *got to go.* Most effective when used after raking in a huge pot that you've won on the river.

lmao *laughing my ass off.* A more passionate expression of **lol.** Those who believe in peppering their language with expletives may use **lmgdao,** or **lmfao. rotf** — *rolling on the floor* — is often used as a prefix.

lol *laughing out loud.* Sometimes a response to something that is actually funny, or to something not so funny, like a perceived bad beat, or that third full house you've drawn to in the last ten minutes.

nh *nice hand.* Is often meant sarcastically. Irony can be a difficult thing to recognize in cyberspace. **vnh** — *very nice hand* — can seem a little more sincere.

omg *oh my god.* An exclamation of surprise, usually in response to a horrible play by an opponent.

ty *thank you.* Can be the best way to end an argument. Or to start one. **tyvm** when you really mean it.

wtf Because sometimes you just have to say, *what the fuck?*

Every site seems to have built-in language filters to block obscenities, but you can get creative with spacing when you need to call someone an asshole. Most also give you the ability to "mute" the most annoying players.

VIRTUAL RAILBIRDS

Every veteran player has at some time or another encountered "railbirds," the groupies of the poker world, named for their habit of hanging onto the rail to watch a game. Some are fans of the players involved. Many others are broke—if they had money, they'd be playing—and will not hesitate to ask you for a loan.

Professional poker players have a reputation for generosity toward their fellow professionals, helping to keep one another bankrolled during the bad luck spells. Lending money to a railbird, on the other hand, is almost always a mistake.

Amazingly enough, railbirds have crossed over into cyberspace. Every once in a while a player will pop into the chat box, asking his or her fellow players, who are usually complete strangers, for a $20 stake. Whether or not this approach has ever worked, even once, remains a mystery.

KEEPING RECORDS

Now that you're playing online poker, it's time to start keeping some records. There are several good reasons for doing so.

Poker winnings are taxable, of course, but can be offset by your losses (as well as other potential deductions like travel, lodging, and whatever you paid for this book). If you're ever unlucky enough to get audited, you'll be happy to have documented your sessions.

You may also be interested in figuring out some of your poker statistics. Are you really a consistent winner? How much do you make per hour? Does the time of day affect your play? Which games are you absolutely crushing? Which leave you gasping for air? Examining your statistics can help you to discover trends, good and bad.

Finally, there's something innate to record-keeping that encourages you to be a more responsible player. You may find yourself less inclined to make a crying call on the river or play Q-10 out of position if you know you're going to have to document that loss at the end of the session.

You can buy a small notebook (which you can also use to make notes about your regular opponents), set up a spreadsheet in Microsoft Excel©, or use one of a growing number of software products designed to help you keep track of your play—there's currently a Web site called Poker Charts (*www.pokercharts.com*) that will let you log, chart, and analyze your results for free. While becoming intimately acquainted with your actual long-term track record can be a shock to your poker ego, you'll ultimately be happy that you did.

♥ ♦ ♣ ♠ ♥ ♦ ♣ ♠ ♥ ♦ ♣ ♠ ♥ ♦ ♣ ♠ ♥ ♦ ♣ ♠ ♥ ♦ ♣ ♠

YOUR DEFINING MOMENT

You log on to FullTiltPoker.com under the pseudonym "Tommy's Grandma" and sit down at a table, ready for some action. It's $3/6 hold'em for you this afternoon, at least until your boss gets back to the office. You should have a good uninterrupted hour of "work" ahead of you.

You quickly scan the lobby and find three tables currently in action:

	Table		
	#1	#2	#3
# of players	9	8	8
Average Pot	$37	$28	$22
% Seeing the Flop	29%	37%	35%
Hands/Hr	72	100	136

Based solely on the statistics, which table would you choose and why?

♥ ♦ ♣ ♠ ♥ ♦ ♣ ♠ ♥ ♦ ♣ ♠ ♥ ♦ ♣ ♠ ♥ ♦ ♣ ♠ ♥ ♦ ♣ ♠

THE ANSWER

While table #1 (and its $37 pots) and table #2 (boasting the most players per flop) might look tempting, you should clearly sit at table #3.

With 35 percent of the players seeing each flop, there are on average three players participating in each hand. So how do the pots get to $22? Let's imagine what one of these average hands might look like . . .

Three players calling a $3 bet before the flop makes $9. Maybe two of those players will connect with the flop, each calling another $3 bet, or $15 total. If one of these players bets $6 on the turn, we're up to $21, just about our average pot size.

Notice that there hasn't been a single raise! This is clearly a very passive game. You are an aggressive player, and as we know, aggressive players will murder passive games.

As an added bonus, the high number of hands per hour indicates that these players are paying very close attention to the table and acting quickly. Your "earn rate" should ultimately reflect the fact that you'll get to play almost as many hands in an hour at this table as you could at the other two combined.

When you're playing online and don't have the ability to see and gauge the play and mental competency of your opponents, the lobby statistics can be one of the most useful resources in helping you to choose the most profitable game.

7

THE CARDROOM

Man, has poker changed.

Ask a player from an earlier generation to describe the poker scene, and you'll probably hear stories about Texas roadhouses, the backroom of a candy store or after-hours games in the caddyshack at a local golf club. If you were lucky enough to live in a state like California, where poker has long been treated as a legal game of skill, and didn't mind inhaling several metric tons of secondhand smoke, you could test your mettle against a few cold-blooded retirees and shady characters with dubious nicknames like "Artichoke Joe." Otherwise, you were going to have to wait for that trip to Reno or Las Vegas (or Monte

Carlo or Macao) to enter a "professional" gaming establishment.

Today, if you live in the United States, you are likely within driving distance of a full-service cardroom. Some offer gourmet meals, prepared by celebrity chefs. Many are smoke-free. You'll still find your share of shady characters, but they'll be playing alongside successful (and unsuccessful) businesspeople, college students and housewives, even famous actors and actresses.

There are some very good reasons to play in a cardroom. Depending on your area, you're likely to find a variety of games and limits to suit your mood and bankroll. Most of them have state-of-the-art security cameras and professional dealers, making cheating nearly impossible. Perhaps best of all is the chance to escape your circle of regulars and wage psychological warfare (or simply partake in some old-fashioned social interaction) with a diverse cast of characters.

The visit to a cardroom is a must for any serious poker player. Before you jump in the car, however, you might want to consider a few of the disadvantages of casino play. Smaller rooms may not be able to offer a wide selection of games. You're likely to face more serious players representing a tougher challenge than your usual Friday night lineup. And then there are those pesky extra costs—tipping and the rake—that can add up over the course of a session (more on that later).

WHAT TO WEAR

Poker used to be a game that had its own sense of fashion. The original riverboat gamblers were men of style. Perhaps the prototype was Jimmy Fitzgerald, an Irish poker player who, according to Old West historian Robert K. DeArment, traveled up and down the Mississippi porting a wardrobe containing two dozen expensive suits (actually, his three slaves were doing most of the porting), the latest custom-made boots from Paris, and a cascading watch chain some sixteen feet long made of gold spun as thick as his pinkie finger.

The tradition carried on through the 1970s, upheld by such luminaries as Texan Crandall Addington, whose fine play (he placed second in the World Series of Poker in 1978) never interfered with his finer threads—he was known to change his linen suits, silk shirts, designer ties (never loosened), and mink Stetson hats as often as three times a day. Even among the less sartorially splendid players there were certain—let's call them stylistic choices—that could be counted on. Cowboy hats, plaid sports jackets made from potentially hazardous materials, huge pinkie rings, and half-chewed cigars were all *de rigueur*.

While it's hard to believe, fashion in poker has gotten *worse*. The uniform of today's typical Vegas pro seems to consist of ratty sweats, sunglasses, and a baseball cap. The number of slobs you'll see in a poker tournament defies any rational explanation. Paul Magriel, for example, better known to fans of the World Poker Tour as "X-22," has been a National Science Fellow, a chess and backgammon champion, and an Ivy League professor.* When it comes to his wardrobe, however, let's just say that the promotional T-shirts given out at many tournaments actually allow Paul to improve his appearance.

What you do wear goes a long way toward defining your table image. While there's no reason why you can't approach the game with your own sense of style, certain choices do have their virtues.

SUNGLASSES

They say that the eyes are the windows to the soul. The best poker players know this and will stare you down, looking for you to betray your hand with the slightest twitch or blink. Many players will protect themselves from this kind of scrutiny with sunglasses. Some go for sporty (Chris Ferguson's black Oakleys), others opt for elegant (Johnny Chan's black-and-gold Versaces), and some choose straight-up psychedelic (Scottie Nguyen's purple-tinted shades).

One important thing to keep in mind: Wearing sunglasses at the final table of the World Series can give you the look and edge of a champion. Those same sunglasses at a $2/4 table will probably make you look like a jackass. If you're ever fortunate enough to make the final table of a World Poker Tour event, you'll find that the producers are quite aware of the "jackass" factor and have outlawed sunglasses. Everyone watching on the Travel Channel will get to see the look of fear in your eyes (a false tell, of course) when Phil Hellmuth Jr. stares into your soul, contemplating a raise.

---

* The nickname "X-22" apparently comes from a 64-player chess tournament Magriel waged against himself. X-22 won.

HATS

Just as with sunglasses, a good hat can help hide your face during those gut-wrenching showdowns. The ubiquitous baseball cap is effective, but has almost become cliché. Cowboy hats work best if you're actually from someplace where cowboys still roam. Fishing caps are popular and have a lot of metaphorical significance in a game where "fish" and "fishing" play significant roles. Perhaps the most famous lid of all time was the Lincolnesque stovepipe that Ken "Top Hat" Smith, a utilities contractor and chess master from Dallas, wore to the 1978 World Series. After each winning hand, Smith would tip his cap to the crowd—occasionally while standing on the table—and declare "What a player!" (He finished sixth.)

COMFORTABLE CLOTHES

Poker is a game of sitting relatively motionless for long periods of time . . . interrupted by adrenaline-filled moments of absolute terror. As a result, you'll see very few poker players wearing knotted ties, turtlenecks, crotch-hugging jeans, or any other potential source of discomfort. (Actually, when you do come across a player who's relaxed enough to wear a tie without loosening it, you're looking at someone who isn't too worried about losing money, likely a maniac, a top-notch player, or both. Be afraid, be very afraid.)

Some players favor hooded sweatshirts, hoping to further conceal their features from scrutiny. One guy who may have taken this look too far is Phil Laak, whose hood-and-dark glasses approach has earned him the nickname "Unabomber."

Most pros, however, dress for comfort. Phil Ivey has a seemingly infinite collection of sports jerseys. Paul Darden decks himself out in Phat Farm sweats. Dewey Tomko always looks prepared to make a quick transition to the nearest golf course.

Other players have taken the notion of comfort to ridiculous extremes. Some players play barefoot. It's unlikely that poker will ever institute a dress code, but there should at least be a rule of thumb about the number of holes a T-shirt can have or how many times it can be worn (how about once?) without being washed. At least consider "Casual Friday" as a guide, especially if you're going to be on TV.

If you are a superstitious person, you may be forced to develop your own fashion code. T. J. Cloutier develops relationships with certain shirts. "I wore a blue terrycloth dress shirt at the Bicycle the first year I won it, so I brought it back the next year, and I won it again. Then I brought it back the next year and I won it again. Then, somehow," he confesses, laughing, "it was too old to wear anymore."

OTHER ACCOUTREMENTS

Stop by the $10/20 table at Hollywood Park and more likely than not, seated to the dealer's right, will be a very large man named "Briz." You'll know it's him because, jutting just above the edge of the rail, looming behind his cards, a huge gold belt buckle—BRIZ—will be staring back at you. The message is clear. Tangle with Briz at your own risk.

Susie Isaacs, a fine poker player with a somewhat questionable sense of fashion—i.e., outfits and hats covered with pictures of playing cards—has developed her own line of "designer gaming jewelry." Whether this is a blessing or a further descent into the depths of kitsch is up to you to decide.

Some people have lucky socks. Others wear good luck medallions, New Age crystals, or enough gold jewelry to rival Mr. T. In the end, you should wear whatever makes you feel like a winner. Because in poker, it's definitely more important to feel good than to look good. As Chris Ferguson, winner of the 2000 World Series, correctly advises, "You can bring your favorite teddy bear to the table if it makes you feel lucky. Just don't blame the teddy bear if your luck turns around."

THE PRICE OF ADMISSION

Casinos are—and should be—in the business of making money. In those games that are played against "the House," the path to profitability is clear. Play roulette and, on average, you'll give back 5 percent more than you'll win. A blackjack player using "perfect strategy" can narrow the odds considerably, but will still be a moderate loser in the long run.

The poker table, however, forces the House into the far less profitable position of impartial observer. To keep the lights on and the dealers dealing, cardrooms have to take a cut from the players.

THE RAKE

While some casinos charge an hourly fee to play at their tables, most accrue their profits in the form of a rake, a small fee removed from every pot. The size of the rake can vary depending on the locale and type of game, but typically tends to be $3 to $5 per deal.

This may not seem like a lot when you're taking down a $200 pot, but the rake adds up over time. Let's say that your local cardroom deals about forty hands an hour, taking an average of $3 from every pot. That's $120 that will disappear from the table every hour. If there are eight players at your table, each of you is paying, on average, $15/hour for the privilege to play in the game.

Thus you'll often hear poker players talk about "beating the rake." To be a consistent winner in the hypothetical game described above, you not only have to be better than your opponents, but you have to be at least $15/hour better. If you're playing for pure entertainment, it's not much more expensive than a movie. But if you're a would-be rounder attempting to grind out a living, the rake can be a serious hindrance to paying the rent.

Beating the rake is an unavoidable part of the casino game. Here are a few things you should keep in mind:

- **Do the math.** Find out how much the rake is before you start playing. The rake makes some low-stakes games (i.e., $2/4 or $3/6) nearly impossible to beat unless you are absolutely dominating the competition.

- **Play fewer hands.** Yes, the table is losing money to the house, but there's no reason why you have to pay your fair share. The more pots you get involved in, the more you end up contributing to the hourly drain. Every hand you don't play is money saved. In other words, tight play becomes even more important in a raked game. Let the maniac who gets involved in every hand take the brunt of it.

- **Smaller can be better.** Cardrooms will often reduce, and in some cases even eliminate, the rake in games that are less than full. If your table suddenly becomes short-handed, ask the dealer if they'll consider a discount.

- **Play higher stakes.** A $5/pot rake at a $3/6 table seems downright oppressive, but the same rake might seem bearable at a $15/30 table, where pots are typically played for hundreds of dollars. It's generally accepted that if you're treating poker as a source of income, you have to be playing at least $10/20 to have a shot at consistently beating the rake. This is tricky advice to follow, however, as the level of competition tends to increase along with the stakes.

TIPPING

The last "hidden cost" of cardroom poker is tipping, which can be a somewhat controversial subject for some players (and most dealers!).

Those in favor say that poker dealers are part of a low-paying service industry that is a lot like waiting tables. Opponents of tipping reply with something like, "Tough nuts! They get a salary, don't they? And besides, she's been dealing me nothing but **rags** all night!"

According to a recent study, poker dealers in southern Nevada are paid an average salary of $6.12/hour, around a dollar more than the state minimum wage. This isn't very much for a job that requires a decent amount of skill (just think about how many "misdeals" take place in an average home game) and the wherewithal to remain calm while angry players pelt them with curses, insults—even cards! In other words, the question isn't whether to tip, but how much. It's ultimately a matter of personal preference, but a dollar per pot won seems to be about the norm.

While you shouldn't feel compelled to tip those dealers who are rude or incompetent, keep in mind that being on the receiving end of awful cards has absolutely nothing to do with the dealer. Really. It doesn't.

"BAD BEAT" JACKPOTS

There are few worse feelings in life (well, poker, anyway) than a bad beat. To help combat the resulting despair, many casinos have added a "bad beat jackpot"—a payout, usually in the thousands (if not tens of thousands) to the unlucky loser of a big hand versus big hand showdown. The requirements are specific to each casino, but are usually along the line of aces full getting cracked by a better aces full, four of a kind, or a straight flush.

Most of these jackpots also provide some extra financial remuneration to the already lucky winner, to everyone seated at the table and, by extension, the dealer, who can generally expect a hefty tip for demonstrating such prowess as to have dealt the hands in the first place. When a jackpot possibility arises—like three aces on the flop (giving aces full to anyone with a pocket pair)—the excitement is often palpable, the whisper "jackpot hand" speeding around the table like electricity.* When the hole cards are turned over, the players will erupt in celebration—or mutter about the one that got away.

Bad beat jackpots have a mixed reputation among poker players. Gamblers love them, as the chance to come home from a low-stakes game with ten grand aligns neatly with their reason for living. More conservative players, however, curse them, recognizing that the house is not providing this service out of some sympathy for battered players. The casino funds the jackpot by taking an extra

---

* Actually, you need to be careful what you say, even if you're whispering. Many cardrooms reserve the right to negate a bad beat jackpot if anyone actually mentions it while the hand is in play.

dollar or so (in addition to the rake) out of every pot. And just like the state lottery, the house is under no obligation to include all of this money in the actual prize pool. In other words, it's another chance for the casino to skim money from the players.

Like them or not, they do exist, and they are a lot of fun to win. They also create the phenomenon known as *bad beat jackpot odds.* Say you're up against what you're pretty sure is aces full, but you've got one card in the deck that will make you a straight flush. While the pot alone will rarely give you enough incentive to chase that card, the size of the bad beat jackpot will more likely than not give you whatever odds you need to make the call.

The casinos, of course, recognize that the existence of the jackpot encourages players to hang around with more speculative hands in the hopes of a miracle card, building bigger pots, creating larger rakes, and—you guessed it— allowing them to skim even more money off the players.

PLAYERS' REVENGE: COMPS AND CLUBS

Fortunately for the player, that old-time free market competition has its rewards. Most casinos know you can just as easily go across the street (or to an online poker site), and they have instituted all kinds of loyalty and rewards programs to keep you coming back.

Some will refund your rake if you play a certain number of hours a month. Others offer "points" that you can exchange for food, lodging, clothing (as long as you don't mind wearing clothing embroidered with the casino's logo), even travel coffee mugs and binoculars. Cardrooms will

often host lotto-style giveaways—for prizes like new cars—
or freerolls, poker tournaments without any entry fees.

Hardly the fabled free lunch, but it's as close as you're
likely to get. If you're going to play with any regularity at a
particular cardroom, the three minutes or so it takes to
sign up will be time well spent.

THE FIRST TRIP TO THE CARDROOM

Walking into a cardroom for the first time can be a pretty
intimidating experience. Poker's recent surge in popularity
has made getting a seat more difficult than dining in a four-
star restaurant (expect to wait at least an hour for a spot at the
Bellagio on a Friday night) and has created veritable mob
scenes near the door. What follows will be old hat for experienced players, but may save some aggravation for first-timers.

When you enter the poker room, your first stop will be
the **board,** where you can sign up for a table. In some
rooms, the board is literally a board; in others, it's more
like the reservation clipboard at a restaurant. Most actually take reservations if you call ahead, something to consider if you're looking to play during peak hours. Keep in
mind as well that rooms are often divided into high-limit
and low-limit sections, each with their own board.

The **host** will take your initials (or your first name and last
initial) and call you when the seat you've requested is available. Unless they happen to be your actual initials, giving
"AA" to the host is neither original nor particularly clever. If
you're planning to step outside to smoke a cigarette, use the
facilities, or sneak in a few hands of blackjack, tell the host to
"lock up your seat," which will buy you a couple of minutes if

your name gets called and you're not around to hear it. There are those times when the wait is so unbearable that you might be tempted to slip the host a discreet bribe. Sometimes it actually works; use your judgment here.

Once you are called, you'll be directed to the **floorman,** who will escort you to your seat. Floormen may be the most important people to befriend in a cardroom, as they know the flavor of every game going and are the final arbiters in all table disputes. A "friendly" floorman will direct you to the center seat at a table full of fish and take pains to see your side in any argument. Occasionally they can be counted on to help you find a seat on very crowded nights, or to reward your friendship with small perks like VIP parking. Hint: Tipping is a very good way to make friends.

After you take your seat, a chip runner will take your money and return with chips. Most players like to buy in for a **rack** (one hundred chips) of whatever denomination is in play; aggressive players will buy two. Tipping the chip run- ner for the buy-in isn't strictly necessary, but if you later ask him or her to "color you up"—that is, exchange your full racks of chips for a smaller number in a higher denomina- tion—it's common courtesy to stick an extra chip into the rack. As for your physical bankroll, it's a lot more intimidat- ing to buy into a game with hundreds peeled off a roll than it is to pull a stack of ATM-fresh twenties out of your wallet.

The **dealer** may be the most unfairly maligned profes- sion on the planet. The upside is that years of being unfairly blamed for events far beyond the control of mere mortals has helped many of them to develop a clever, self- deprecating wit that is all their own. Whether you find a dealer to be an innocent bystander to the whims of fate or

a vile spawn of some lower level of hell whose sole pur-
pose is to separate you from your chips is a good indica-
tion of your character as a poker player.

One of the many burdens faced by these professionals is
that while they will do all of the manual labor of shuffling,*
passing out and collecting the cards, and regulating the
betting, the title of "dealer" is actually reserved for one of
the players! (Perhaps poker dealers deserve their own
unique nickname, like "card mediums" or "punching bags.")
This player/dealer—whose reign is commemorated by a
white plastic disc called the button—gets the advantage (as
discussed in Chapter Three) of being one of the last people
to act during the pre-flop betting and the last person to act
on every subsequent round of betting. This is the equivalent of prime real estate for poker players, who covet good
position the way that some people long for an ocean view.

The button bestows its magnificent powers for only a
single hand before moving, clockwise, to the next player at
the table. For purposes of clarity, from here on out we'll
call this person "the button," saving the term "dealer" for
the person who shuffles and deals the cards.

If you're sitting down to a new game, the dealer will
deal one card, face up, to each player. The player with the
highest card—aces are tops, ties are broken by appealing
to the suits, which are ranked, from highest to lowest,
spades, hearts, diamonds, and clubs—wins the button for
the inaugural deal.

If you are joining a game in progress, you are going to

---

* In some places, this task has been taken away from the dealers by automated
shuffling machines. It's not a move meant to stem cheating; rather the intention is to speed up play—the more hands that are dealt, the more rakes the
House can collect.

have to **post a blind** before you can participate in a hand. While you can post a blind from any position except the button, most players will wait until it's their turn to be the big blind (a bet that they would have had to make anyway) or the button has made its way to the player on their immediate left (ensuring that this forced bet can at least benefit from the best possible position). Posting a blind from anywhere else generally marks a player as a rube or someone too impatient to wait the five minutes or so for a better spot to get involved in the action—in other words, the kind of person who causes experienced players to salivate.

"BURN AND TURN"

Watch a professional poker dealer, and you'll see her "burn" the top card in the deck, throwing it face down into the muck, before dealing the flop, turn, and river.

It's not just a quirky habit, but a longstanding measure to discourage cheating. An unscrupulous card marker might be able to deduce the identity of the "burn" card before it's dealt, but the actual "turn" card remains safely hidden from view.

While you're unlikely to encounter marked cards in a casino, it's nice to know that you're being protected.

THE CARDROOM BILL OF RIGHTS

There are a good many idiosyncrasies in casino poker that may differ from your home game. Failure to understand them may result in some expensive mistakes and/or penalties, so know your rights!

THE RIGHT TO PROTECT YOUR CARDS

Dealers are under a lot of pressure to deal as many hands as they can. As a result, they will sometimes mistakenly sweep a "live" hand into the **muck,** the black hole of the poker table. You can complain all you want to the floorman, but once your cards touch any of the other cards in the muck, they are, without ifs, ands, or buts, dead.

As a poker player, however, you do have the right to protect your hole cards by placing something on top of them. Most players use a chip. More creative or superstitious types, however, have been known to protect their cards with all kinds of talismans, statuettes, lucky crystals, etc.

Just remember that while abstinence may be the best way to avoid losing money, if you do decide to play, use protection.

THE RIGHT TO A NEW DECK

During the course of play, dealers are regularly supplied with new "setups," poker talk for two brand-new decks of cards. If you don't like the deck that's in play, you have the right to ask the dealer to use the other one. If the other one has already been used, you can ask for a new setup.

It's a rule that once made a lot of sense before the advent of professional dealers (yes, players used to deal their own hands) and security cameras. Now it's mainly used by superstitious players who don't like the way their luck is running. Players who aren't as superstitious mainly get annoyed by these requests. When a dealer gets a new setup, he or she has to spread both decks out on the table, examining each to insure that all of the cards are there, before shuffling and dealing can resume. It's a time-consuming business. In an attempt to mitigate the willy-nilly abuse of this rule, most rooms will make you wait until a new deck has made a full orbit around the table before you can request another one.

THE RIGHT TO A NEW SEAT

When, during the course of a game, a seat opens up at your table, you have the right to move to it. Depending on the position of the button, you may be forced to re-post one or both of the blinds.

While this is an action usually inspired by a superstitious belief in "hot" or "cold" seats, there are sometimes some very good reasons for moving. When there's a maniac at the table, experienced players will usually want to sit directly to their left (where they can raise the maniac's reckless bets in an attempt to drive out the rest of the field with a double-bet) or to their right (where they can see how everyone else at the table responds to the maniac's action before deciding on their own course). It's also a good way to get away from people whose smoking, body odor, or incessant chatter is starting to get to you.

THE RIGHT TO LOOK AT ANOTHER PLAYER'S CARDS

You have the right to ask to see any hand that, once play has ended, hasn't been folded. It's considered bad form, however, to make such requests with any regularity—allowing your opponents to lose with dignity isn't just common courtesy, it's good poker.

There's also nothing illegal about sneaking a peek if the person sitting next to you is careless in the way he or she looks at her cards, a trait especially common among the very elderly and the very drunk. A good rule of thumb if someone is repeatedly exposing his hole cards to you is to offer up a single warning. After that it's fair game.

SOME RIGHTS THAT YOU DON'T HAVE
THE RIGHT TO SPLASH THE POT

You'll recall the climactic showdown in *Rounders*, where Teddy KGB makes a bet by tossing a handful of chips into the center of the table. Mike McDermott, his opponent, asks him to stop "splashing the pot." To which Teddy replies, "It's my club, and I can splash the pot any time I damn well please."

In most cardrooms, however, you cannot splash the pot any time you damn well please, or ever, for that matter, as it's very difficult to discern exactly how much money is being tossed in there. When you're looking to add chips to the pot, just place them in front of you, allowing the dealer to verify the size of the bet before sweeping them into the middle.

THE RIGHT TO STRING BET

A devious poker player will do whatever possible to extract information from his or her fellow players. One way of doing this is to call a bet, take a quick look around the table to see how people react, then reach back into his or her stack to pull out a raise.

This is called a **string bet,** and it's illegal in almost every cardroom. If you want to raise, you need to do it in one distinct action. You can also say "raise" (hopefully in a voice that exudes confidence in your hand) before pushing any of your chips forward, giving you free license to go back and forth to your stack at will before committing to an amount.

THE RIGHT TO ANNOUNCE YOUR HAND

In a recent World Poker Tour event, Paul "Dot.com" Phillips faced an all-in raise from his sole opponent, Mel Judah. Attempting to extract some clue to the nature of Judah's hand, Phillips announced his own: "I've got a flush, Mel."

While Phillips's action went unpunished in the moment it occurred, commentator Mike Sexton correctly pointed out that what he had done was a violation of tournament rules. You aren't allowed to reveal your hand, whether verbally or physically, while it's in play.

CHEATING

In the mid-1970s, four California draw poker players became quite proficient at duping their opponents at the $30/60 table out of a little extra money. It went a little something like this:

Mr. Grey (not his real name, of course) looks down at his

cards to find three aces, a huge starting hand in draw poker. He fans his cards, slightly repositioning his thumb, and opens with a $30 raise.*

Unaware of the web of deceit surrounding them, a couple of unlucky players call. The action gets to Mr. Pink, who, having picked up on Mr. Grey's subtle signal, re-raises to $60 with whatever junk cards he happens to be holding. A third player, Mr. Yellow, calls the $60 cold. Mr. Grey merely calls the raise, trapping the two pigeons in the middle into calling the second bet.

After the draw, Mr. Grey opens with a bet. The two pigeons call, as does Mr. Pink. Mr. Yellow, however, raises. Mr. Grey calls, the two pigeons call . . . and Mr. Pink raises.

Not only are the two pigeons likely to lose to Mr. Grey's powerhouse hand, but it's going to cost them several extra bets to do so.

Lest the other players at the table get suspicious, Mr. Grey bids his farewell, only to be replaced by Mr. Orange, the fourth co-conspirator, who starts the process all over again.

This colorful team wasn't the only group working this sort of angle. Mr. Grey recalls a time when, intending to play a more legitimate style of poker, he took his seat in a nine-person game. Before he could play his first hand, he was tapped on the shoulder by the floorman, an old friend of his, who invited him to come see the cardroom's new state-of-the-art security system. As they ventured into the privacy of a backroom, the floorman explained that the eight other people at the table were *all* in cahoots, waiting for an unlucky ninth to join their game.

* In this style of California draw, the first player into the pot was obligated to open with a raise.

Needless to say, Mr. Grey found another table. What's troubling about this story is that the floorman—and by extension, the cardroom—not only knew about the cheating, but did nothing to prevent it. In their eyes, action was action, and far be it for them to interfere.

Fortunately, the golden age of cheating has come to an end. After one of these Gardena cardrooms was forced to shut its doors—its notoriety as a haven for cheaters had become so prevalent that the "action" simply stopped coming—the surviving casinos began to realize that they could no longer turn a blind eye to their reputations. Most of today's rooms have "eyes in the sky" and scrupulous floormen who are on the lookout for this kind of activity. You should feel very secure about playing in public cardrooms that are well regulated—the chances that you will be cheated are very, very small. That being said, should you suspect any funny business, get up from the game and find another, discreetly notifying the floorman en route.

OTHER CARDROOM QUIRKS

Nowadays, the rules of hold'em are pretty well etched in stone. Each cardroom, however, has its own idiosyncrasies that you should be aware of.

CAPPED POTS

Most cardrooms limit the number of raises that can be made on any particular street, usually to three (allowing a total of four bets), sometimes four (or five bets total) before the betting is declared capped.

Many rooms dismiss the cap when two players get

heads-up, allowing them to raise and re-raise one another until someone runs out of chips. You can ask the dealer or floorman to explain any rules particular to the table where you're seated.

KILL POTS

Revenge is sweet, an idea that's not lost on some casinos, who use **kill pots** to spice up their games. A player who wins two hands in a row gets the "kill button" and is required to post a bet—usually twice the size of the blind—on the next hand, ostensibly giving everyone else a chance to win some of their money back in a raised pot.

Many opposing players will try to take advantage of the situation by raising, getting three bets into the pot against the guy with the kill button, who has been forced to cough up the double bet with whatever random two cards he's been dealt. What's intriguing, however, is that the player with the kill button is almost always getting decent enough odds to call the raise, setting the stage for another potentially infuriating beat.

STRADDLE RAISES

Every once in a while you'll come across a player who, while sitting under the gun (the seat just to the left of the big blind, whose job it is to open the initial round of betting), likes to post a double-bet before the cards are dealt. By making a **straddle raise,** the player is committing himself—and anyone else who wants to gamble with him—to a raised pot before he's even looked at his cards. It's rarely a very profitable play. Not only are you playing a hand that, more often than not, will be less than premium, but you're committing to playing it from one of the least advantageous positions at the table. But making a straddle raise but can be an extremely effective tool if you're looking to propagate a loose table image or deliver an agonizing bad beat.

THE BEST CARDROOMS IN THE WORLD

BELLAGIO, LAS VEGAS, NEVADA

It's not the largest, but it may be the classiest poker room in the world. On any given night, you're bound to find luminaries like Doyle Brunson, Jen Harman, or Phil Ivey playing in the top section.

BINION'S HORSESHOE,
LAS VEGAS, NEVADA

The venerable Horseshoe has fallen on hard times of late—tax problems recently forced its closure. Harrah's, however, has stepped in to reopen the casino, allowing players to make the pilgrimage to see the Wall of Fame, poker's equivalent of Yankee Stadium.

COMMERCE CASINO,
CITY OF COMMERCE, CALIFORNIA

If poker had a heaven, it might look something like the Commerce Casino. There are more games being spread here, encompassing the full spectrum of limits, than anywhere else in the world.

FOXWOODS,
MASHANTUCKET, CONNECTICUT

The Commerce of the East, the poker room at Foxwoods can hold up to seventy-six separate games at any time.

HONORABLE MENTIONS

AVIATION CLUB DE FRANCE,
PARIS, FRANCE

BAY 101, SAN JOSE, CALIFORNIA

CASINO RAY, HELSINKI, FINLAND

CONCORD CARD CASINO,
VIENNA, AUSTRIA

GROSVENOR VICTORIA CASINO,
LONDON, ENGLAND

HOLLYWOOD PARK CASINO,
INGLEWOOD, CALIFORNIA

TAJ MAHAL, ATLANTIC CITY, NEW JERSEY

INTERMISSION: HOW TO PUT A TABLE ON TILT

Winning a small pot feels good. Winning a huge pot feels great.

Sometimes you'll be lucky enough to sit at a loose table, where maniacs will raise and re-raise your nut hands all the way to the river, spoon-feeding you pot after pot.

Other times you'll find yourself at table full of tight-fisted rocks, folding too early and too often for you to realize anything but the most marginal profits. That is, unless you can transform these models of rational judgment and sober restraint into bloodthirsty, raving lunatics yelling "Cappuccino!" as they toss in their fourth bets.

The easiest way to accomplish this is to put your opponents *on tilt,* exasperating them into committing completely irrational acts, which you then exploit mercilessly.

The following strategies should be wielded with great care. Used properly, they can result in some of your most legendary winning nights. But be warned: Should you try any of these techniques and fail, you will probably look like, well, a complete ass.

DELIVER A BAD BEAT

If you're playing poker "correctly"—that is, calling or betting only when you have the right odds—you're going to suffer more bad beats than you inflict. The theory of **implied tilt odds** (or ITO), however, suggests that the correct way is not always the best way. ITO relies on the notion that calling a bet when you have no mathematical business doing so, then winning the hand, will leave your stunned opponent muttering obscenities and chasing his money for the rest of the night.

Here's an example: A super-tight player has raised and re-raised with what you (and everyone else at the table) *know* are pocket aces, after you've inexplicably raised from the small blind with 7-2s. The flop comes down A-K-2 with one of your suit. Should you continue with the hand? Odds calculated in the traditional way would say no. The implied tilt odds, however, tell you to go right ahead. Sure, you probably won't make that **runner-runner flush**, or catch running deuces to make quads against his aces full. But those few times that you do will completely destroy your opponent's faith in the natural order of the universe, and should earn you enough angry money over the rest of the session to make this a profitable play.

FEIGN DRUNKENNESS

Nobody likes a drunk. A winning drunk is even worse. Scooping big pots while seemingly intoxicated to the point of near-collapse is a sure way to piss off your opponents.

Order a drink. Say "another drink" even if it's your first. Spill a little on your lap—never underestimate the sense of smell—and alternate between holding your head miserably in your hands and erupting in fits of delirious, high-pitched giggles.

This style of play is not recommended if you actually *are* drunk, in which case you should probably tighten up your play considerably, or, better yet, sleep it off. If you're of that rare breed who actually plays *better* drunk, congratulations! You've got a natural edge.

BECOME A BULLY

Admit it. There have been times when you were pushed around by somebody stronger, smarter, or just meaner than you. Remember how you felt? Now imagine trying to play poker in that state.

Choose an opponent to pick on. Men with recently loosened ties are often your best bet, but you should select your target according to your ability to annoy certain personality types. Taunt them at every opportunity, mixing emotional torture ("Wow, that one had to hurt") with observational humor ("When did you decide to get the hair plugs?").

Then wait for an opportunity to "lie" about your hand. For example, when you're pretty sure your target has something like two pair, offer a warning like, "Don't call, I've got a flush!" When they make the crying call, turn over your full house. You will see the steam coming out of their ears.*

Bullying doesn't work on everyone, but when you find someone who gets easily offended at the poker table, it can be your best (and most perversely satisfying) weapon.

"SLOWROLLING"

Taking an unnecessarily long time to announce, analyze, or otherwise evaluate your opponent's second-best hand before turning over your winning cards—or, as they say, "slowrolling"—is a great way to make enemies at the table. This play is especially effective against old crocodiles who already resent you for being such a moronic young whippersnapper.

UNLEASH YOUR INNER ANNOYING SELF

For some, the ability to fill the air with incessant, meaningless chatter comes naturally. For others, it's an acquired skill. If you have it, nurture it. If you don't, start studying the behavioral patterns of annoying people. A distracted player is a losing player, and you want to provide as much distraction as possible.

Talk about your troubles with your girlfriend. Or your boyfriend. Or your girlfriend's boyfriend. Bemoan life

---

* Yes, revealing your hand is illegal, but there's technically nothing to prevent you from *lying* about your hole cards.

with your stepkids (real or imagined). Comment on your every move: "I guess I just have to call." Hum. Develop facial tics. Pass gas.

The trick is to create a general aura of annoyance without getting people so aggravated that they leave the table.

PRESTO!

A variant of the bad beat, wielding the power of Presto is a skill that takes a moment to learn and a lifetime to master. All you have to do is win a hold'em hand with pocket fives, declaring "Presto!" as you turn over your cards.* One's level of Presto expertise is determined by just how bad a beat gets delivered, i.e., flopping a set of fives against pocket aces is good, but gut-shotting a straight on the river represents the work of a true Presto master.

An added benefit: Once you've introduced Presto to a table, some if not all of your opponents are going to join in, creating a lot of "dumb" money.

STUDY ASIAN HISTORY

An old Chinese proverb describes a little gambling as "soothing and relaxing." Gambling has been a respectable part of Asian life since early history, so it's no surprise that the region has produced a rich cultural tradition of delivering bad beats with unique style and panache. Whether it's phrases like "Cha Ching!" and "Ai-yah!" or more physical expressions like karate chopping the table and standing up on a chair, many of the Asian greats have an uncanny ability to put their opponents on tilt. Study them carefully.

---

* It's customary to acknowledge another player's successful Presto by responding with your own cry of "Erwin!"

THE TILTBOYS

In the mid-1990s, a group of friends gathered around the shared principle of "angling"—pulling fast ones on other people and, as often as possible, on each other—in the hopes of pushing them over the edge of rational behavior. The "Tiltboys," as we called ourselves, took frequent trips to Las Vegas, Reno, San Bruno, or any other place where we could find a poker game and a steady stream of opportunities to place side bets on everything from the over/under on the total hours we'd sleep to the number of times I'd be rejected while trying to flirt with a woman at the table.

Getting angled by a fellow Tiltboy, whether by a "schneiding" on the river or a tough loss at golf, Roshambo, or the "Circle Game," would cause your level of anger—measured on the Tiltmeter—to rise, a condition that could only be cured by a successful angling of your own.

The only thing more fun than driving a fellow Tiltboy to a full head of steam might have been the opportunities to put complete strangers on megatilt. Like the time Dave "Dice Boy" Lambert—also nicknamed "Six Sigma Man" for his propensity to luck out far more often than what any statistician could conceivably describe as normal—inflicted a series of ridiculously bad beats on *Cardplayer* magazine columnist Roy Cooke at a $20/40 table. Or when we "skirted" the rules of a women's only tournament at Bay 101 by appearing in drag. (Transformed Tiltgirl Michael "Michelle" Stern took down a share of first place!)

If any of this seems intriguing, or if you're just a fan of really immature male behavior, several essays chronicling the exploits of the Tiltboys—including rare photos of "Phyllis" Gordon in a light magenta frock and a blue straw hat with a white chiffon ribbon—can be found at www.tiltboys.com.

YOUR DEFINING MOMENT

It's Wednesday afternoon, about one P.M., and your boss pokes his head into your cubicle to tell you that he's got a business meeting that will keep him out of the office for the rest of the afternoon. Ten minutes after he leaves, you're on your way to the local cardroom for some $15/$30 hold'em.

No names on the sign-up list, so you walk directly to the table, where an open seat is waiting for you. You pull $500 from your wallet, call for the chip runner, and . . . oops. There's your boss, sitting on your right.

He gives you a little smirk. "I didn't get the memo. Were you invited to this meeting?" You both have a good laugh.

But the laughs are over when, a few hands later, your boss raises to $30 from under the gun. You look down to find [K♣] [Q♣]. Quickly scanning the table, you notice that the woman in the small blind has already peeked at her cards and seems very interested in the action.

Are you going to three-bet your boss or **smooth call** his raise and see the flop?

Well, job security is certainly an issue. But business is business — this is poker. You really want to play this hand heads-up, in position. That means eliminating the woman in the small blind.

You three-bet. The small blind pauses, thinks, then reluctantly calls. So much for isolating your boss, who, of course, calls the bet as well. Three-way action, with $150 in the pot.

The flop comes down, [10♣] [9♠] [4♦]. The small blind checks, your boss bets $15.

Your play, your Defining Moment.

♥ ♦ ♣ ♠ ♥ ♦ ♣ ♠ ♥ ♦ ♣ ♠ ♥ ♦ ♣ ♠ ♥ ♦ ♣ ♠ ♥ ♦ ♣ ♠ ♥ ♦ ♣ ♠

THE ANSWER

There is now $165 in the pot. With four jacks left in the deck—or so you hope—and forty-seven cards unknown, you have about a 1 in 12 chance of turning a jack. The pot is giving you 11-to-1 odds, so clearly you must play. Instead of just calling, however, you decide that the better play—not for your career, but for the pot—is to raise. You'll almost certainly force the small blind to (finally) fold, and in all likelihood you'll get a "free" look at the turn card.

You raise. The small blind folds and your boss calls. You figure him for A-10.

The turn brings the [5♥ ♥]. Your boss checks. Your plan is working, and there's no reason to deviate from it now. There is no way your boss can fold a pair at this point, so you check and take your "free" shot at the river.

B-I-N-G-O! The river brings the [J♥]. Your boss fires $30 at the pot. But you have the immortal nuts. You're the boss now, and the boss has to raise. He makes the crying call, you scoop the pot.

"Gotta run, folks. Business meeting in a few minutes," he says as he rises from the table. "Can we expect to see you back at work today?"

"I am at work," you retort, and go about stacking his chips.

8

MOVIN' ON UP

Low-limit hold'em games are the salt mines of the poker world. That's not to say that you can't find plenty of amusement engaging in wild play with often colorful characters. But playing to win can be an incredibly frustrating, boring experience. Let's count the reasons why.

(1) **Loose starting hand requirements.** Did that guy really just call three bets cold with a Q-2 offsuit? Low-limit games are often dominated by players who will start and even raise with all kinds of junk. Poker is most profitable when you're playing in a way that's contrary to your opposition. In other words, to be a consistent winner at low-limit hold'em, you have to tighten up considerably, throwing away the vast majority of your hands while the action players around you seem to get involved in every pot.

(2) **Loose callers.** That same joker who played the Q-2 just called you all the way to the end, turning a 2 and catching a miracle queen on the river to crack your wired kings. These sorts of confounding bad beats can be enough to make you swear off the game (temporarily, at least).

(3) **Tunnel vision.** Many low-limit poker players are asking themselves one basic question: What do I need to make my hand? They couldn't be less concerned with what you're holding, or what you are purporting to hold, making most bluffs against them completely worthless. Low-limit hold'em is a game where you're going to have to show the goods to win the hand, and let's face it, the goods can sometimes be hard to come by.

(4) **The R/E ratio,** or the rake as compared to your earnings. You may be a decent poker player, beating your regular opponents out of a big bet every hour. But if that regular game is $2/4, and the cardroom rakes $3 out of every pot, you may actually be losing money over the long run.*

Some poker books advise new players to escape the hell that is low-limit poker as quickly as possible. This is *not* one of those books.

A good poker player can beat just about any low-limit game. If you are not consistently beating the madmen and morons at the $3/6 table, you are probably not going to be able to succeed at the middle-limits.

Here's the good news: If you are beating your low-limit game, you're about to have one of those Mr. Miyagi "wax on, wax off" moments from *The Karate Kid*. All of that drudgery has actually prepared you for better things in ways that you might not have realized:

---

* Some poker theoreticians will tell you that these kinds of games are "unbeatable." However, they are generally populated by players who are so willing to throw their money away that your rate should be significantly higher than a big bet an hour, compensating for the horrendous rake.

(1) **Loose starting hand requirements.** Learning how to throw away hand after hand is one of the most valuable skills you can master. Patience is more than just a virtue at the poker table—it's necessary for your very survival.

(2) **Loose callers.** If you've been paying attention during all of those bad beats, then you've surely started to develop a sort of sixth sense for knowing when you're in trouble. Some call it poker ESP; the more mundane explanation is that you've simply developed an instinct for reading **board texture** (more on this later) and identifying subtle inconsistencies in the way the hand is being played.

(3) **Tunnel vision.** Without being able to rely on bluffs, you've had to play a very mathematical form of poker, learning how to get your money into the pot when you have the best of it, and the odds of getting there when you don't. You can't be a consistent winner without having mastered this lesson.

(4) **The R/E ratio.** Milking a $3/6 game for a big bet an hour might make you feel good, but beating a $20/40 game at the same rate qualifies as a living wage!

So there you have it, young grasshopper. Succeed in the low-limits, and you will be prepared to excel as you move up through the poker ranks.

WHAT IS A MIDDLE-LIMIT GAME?

The middle-limits are traditionally defined as games ranging from $10/20 to $80/160, that class of games in which you should be prepared to face bankroll swings in the thousands, but not quite tens of thousands.

In terms of actual play, however, the lines are much less clear. There are $3/6 games online that require more thought and skill than some $20/40 games at Hollywood Park. So what separates the relatively highbrow middle-limit game from its less sophisticated cousin? It's like they say about obscenity: You'll know it when you see it.

A middle-limit game will usually feature players who know how to play an A-game. They've read some of the same poker books as you and have spent time away from the table thinking about the game. They don't play too many junk hands, at least not regularly, unless they are trying to fool you into believing that they are the kinds of players who do. They'll study your play, looking for tells and betting patterns, attempting to put you on specific hands. They know the odds and are capable of folding hands when they are convinced they have the worst of it. At the same time, they suspect that you are capable of the same, and will occasionally make fancy plays in the hopes of getting you to do so.

Don't let any of this scare you too much—there's a world of difference between knowing how to play an A-game and doing so with any kind of consistency. You'll still find people who will call with rags, go on tilt, and chase big hands with inadequate pot odds. You are going to charge them for their mistakes.

LEAKS

Every poker player makes mistakes. It's an inevitable part of the game.

The lower-limits and their multiway pots tend to be very forgiving of errors. A few incorrect bets or calls here and there can be quickly swept away by one huge pot. Even on your worst nights, you'll be hard-pressed to lose more than a couple of hundred dollars.

At the middle-limits, a single mistake can cost you a couple of hundred dollars, and there'll be fewer horrible players to help you overcome them. Learning to live with the occasional big loss is part of the game.

The key is to avoid making the same mistake over and over again. Poker players refer to these repeated errors as "leaks" in their game. Some leaks that aren't so noticeable at the lower limits can sink your ship once you reach the middle-limit game. Here are a few:

Overvaluing the almighty ace

A guy sitting next to me who regularly examined his cards one at a time once confessed, "When I look down and find an ace, I try to bet immediately. I'm afraid I'll lose my nerve once I see that other card." Funny, in a sad clown kind of way. Lots of players like to play any ace, forgetting that (a) they only have about an 18 percent of flopping one, and (b) other people like to play aces as well, often with better kickers. Regularly playing ace-junk is a good way to lose regularly.

But they're the same suit!

There's something about the chance of a flush that makes even wizened players go daft. You're only going to flop two of your suit once out of every nine tries, and when you do, you'll only complete that flush one time in three. Even when you do make a flush with, say, your jack-four of spades, you'll be living in fear of a fourth spade appearing on the board to give a better flush to someone holding the ace, king, or queen. The same logic can also be applied to playing small pairs. Those pocket threes are only going to flop trips one time in eight—the remaining seven times, you're probably sunk. If there are only three or four players entering the pot each time, you aren't going to be getting good value on your investment.

Falling in love with premium hands

Pocket aces are rare—once in 221 hands, to be exact—so there's good reason to regard them as a gift from the poker gods. That being said, it's insane to even think about *calling* a bet with [A♠] [A♠] after the flop's come [J♥] [10♥♥] [9♥ ♥] and the action's been capped before it gets to you. Same goes for a hand like pocket kings or queens against an ace-high flop. Clinging too long to a premium hand in the face of obvious danger because you know you're *supposed* to win can be an expensive way to play.

Position, schmosition

Playing ace-suited from early position is probably okay at most low-limit tables but can be a recipe for disaster in a game full of tight, aggressive players who will raise you—and usually beat you—with a better ace. Same goes for hands like J-10 offsuit and wired sixes. Against the tougher players in the middle-limit game, position becomes even more important; failing to account for it can sink your game.

Calling

To quote the *The Three Amigos,* "We all have our El Guapos to face." For some, it's calling too many hands from the small blind ("Of course 9-6 offsuit is a crappy hand, but it's only half a bet!"). For others, it's calling raises from the big blind ("Of course 9-6 offsuit is a crappy hand, but I'm already halfway there!"). It might be your inability to throw those pocket 8s away from the button in the face of a raise and re-raise. Whatever your personal El Guapo might be, keep in mind that calling is the weakest tool in your utility belt of poker moves and can cost you a lot of money over the long haul.

AVOID DOMINATION

Being dominated at the poker table occurs when you share a common card with an opponent—generally a big card—but are holding a second card that leaves you severely "out-kicked." Ace-king, for example, dominates ace-ten. King-jack dominates king-nine.

This isn't as big a deal in the lower limits, where you're playing most of your holdings as if they were drawing hands (i.e., you know you'll probably have to make two pair or a straight to win against a large field of opponents). Many middle-limit battles, however, are waged against only one or two opponents. In a heads-up confrontation, the dominant hand will win 75 percent of the time.

Avoid playing hands that are easily dominated, especially when there's been a raise in front of you. Many good players would rather call an early position raiser with 9-8s than with A-10.

BOARD TEXTURE

One of the most important skills in Texas Hold'em is the ability to evaluate the cards that are on the table, otherwise known as the texture of the board. You've obviously already learned to read the board to figure out the *absolute* value of your hand—i.e., my hand plus the cards on the board give me a flush. What you'll come to realize, however, is that it's much more important to be able to assess the *relative* value of your hand, or where your hand stands in relation to the cards your opponents are probably holding.

Here's a simple example. Let's say that you have K♥ K♦. You raise before the flop from early position, and three people call you. The flop comes

J♠ 10♦ 4♠.

You bet, and all three of your opponents call you. Now let's say the turn card is the

A♠.

Do you see why it would now be right to check your hand and, in the face of any action, fold it immediately? In this case, the A♠ is what poker players call a **death card**, as it's given your opponents three different ways to beat you: You are now drawing dead to anyone holding a K-Q or two spades, and have only two outs against anyone with an ace. Remember that all three of your opponents called you on the flop, making it extremely likely that at least one of them has just pulled ahead of you.

Being able to reassess the value of your hand in relation to the board—and having the discipline to throw it away—is critical to your hold'em success.

Reading board texture isn't all about running away from danger, however. As you'll see in the next section, you'll often be able to benefit from a scary board.

BLUFFING

One of the best (and worst) things about middle-limit hold'em is that bluffing finally becomes an integral part of the game.

The reason for this is simple: In order for a bluff to work, you need to be playing against someone who is observant enough to recognize the hand that you are pretending to have and disciplined enough to lay down a reasonably good hand. It's one of poker's great paradoxes: Bluffing only works against smart players.

Against observant players, you'll find all kinds of places to bluff. The best opportunity is when the turn or river brings your opponent's worst nightmare: a scare card. If he's got pocket queens, it's an ace or a king. If she flopped trips, it's that third (or fourth) flush card.

You don't have to wait for the turn or the river—there are many flops that can be won by a "first to bet" strategy. It's very difficult to call a bet or raise in the face of

or even

if you're not holding a significant piece of the flop in your hand. These kinds of bluffs require tenacity, however, as you need to be prepared to follow up your bet with another on the turn if you sense a weak call on the flop.

You don't have to be that successful for bluffs to be an effective strategy. If you're getting 10-to-1 odds from the pot, your bluff needs to work only one time in eleven for it to be a profitable play.

Keep in mind, however, that the reverse is true—you don't need to pick off too many bluffs to make it profitable to call with a hand that's good, but not great, especially against an unrepentant con artist. As a result, it's usually not a good idea to bluff at huge pots or multiple opponents.

MIDDLE LIMIT HOLD'EM
BY BOB CIAFFONE AND JIM BRIER

Ready to escape the hell of low-limit poker? Buy this book first. You'll find articulate, occasionally humorous advice from two very good poker players on how to adjust your game to the bigger stakes. More useful than the text, however, are the book's nearly five hundred hand quizzes, testing your strategic mettle in various middle-limit hold'em situations. You probably won't get all of them right—you may even disagree with some of the answers—but by studying the authors' thoughtful analysis of each situation, you'll definitely become a stronger player.

JUST BECAUSE YOU'RE PARANOID . . .

. . . doesn't mean that someone isn't watching you. At the middle-limit tables, assume that you are always being studied. Your opponents' observations will fall into two basic categories.

PHYSICAL TELLS

It's hard to know when you've got them, and keeping them out of your game requires dedicated effort. Always remain observant of what you are doing. Do you look down at your chips before you are ready to make a bet? Or lean back in your seat while waiting for someone to decide whether or not to call your made hand? Do you bet quickly when you're bluffing and slowly when you've got the goods?

Experience is probably your best ally against physical tells, as your hand probably won't be trembling—generally a sure sign of a monster hand—after the fourth or fifth thousandth time you've bet into the river. You might also want to get into the habit of not looking at your cards before the flop until the action gets to you. Not only will it be impossible to reveal any clues to the nature of your hand, but you can use the time to scrutinize all of your opponents for their own tells. Same goes for the flop—watch your opponents instead of the cards. You'll have plenty of time later to see if you connected with the board, but you won't get a second chance to see your opponents' *immediate* reactions.

Chris Ferguson, the World Champion in 2000, suggests that self-examination is the best way to discover tells in other people. "By observing my own behavior, the way I react in certain situations, I'm able to recognize those behaviors in other people."

Here are some tells for you to look for, both in yourself and your opponents:*

Leaning Back

Some players have a tendency to lean back in their chairs after making a bet, waiting for you to decide what to do. They usually have made hands.

The Tremble

Shaky hands mean strong hands. If a player's hands tremble as he makes a bet, proceed with caution.

The Strong Move to the Pot

Players who are loud or physically aggressive in their betting are often bluffing, while those who bet as if they were afraid to wake up the person sleeping next to them are generally looking for you to call. As is the case with many tells, strong means weak; weak means strong.

Looking Away

Another example of a strong/weak tell: When a player, after making a bet or raise, looks away from you, she usually has a strong hand. A player who looks directly at you after a bet is likely on a bluff.

Reaching for the Chips

When a player starts to reach for his chips before you've had a chance to act, he's usually trying to scare you into checking your hand. Fire away.

---

* A word of warning: Some players consider themselves amateur thespians, and, if they think you might be observing them, will play the "part" in an attempt to trick you into believing they have a certain tell.

Looking Down at the Chips
Many players unconsciously glance at their chips when they're planning to bet or raise.

Beware of the Speech
Someone who goes out of their way to make a long, pre-pared speech after raising you or betting into you on the river probably has the nuts. "Wow, I can't believe it. I'm just really lucky today," or "If I raise you, will you call?" are typical examples.

Silence Is Golden
A chatty player who suddenly shuts up usually intends to play the hand she's been dealt. This is especially true of players in the blinds, making it a good idea to engage them in conversation whenever possible.

TABLE IMAGE
Your opponents will constantly be trying to assess what kind of player you are. Are you loose and wild, susceptible to dominant hands? Or are you a rock, easily bluffed out of the pot when you're not holding the nuts?

The type of table image you should be striving for is something that is still hotly debated among poker's more prominent thinkers. Some believe that it's best to seem like a tight, thoughtful player, garnering more respect for your raises (thus increasing the odds that your better hands will hold up) while allowing you to slip a few bluffs into the mix. Others argue that you should play the part of the maniac, forcing your opponents to call you all the way to the river to pay off your winning hands.

One thing everyone can agree on is that you don't want

to appear weak. Weak players are bloody chum for the sharks of the poker world.

The best approach is probably to vary your image. This applies both to the types of hands that you play—sometimes it's okay to limp with aces and raise before the flop with your suited 5-3—as well as the way that you play them. Don't fall into obvious betting patterns that reveal too much about the strength of your hand.

ABOUT SHOWING YOUR CARDS . . .

Many professionals *never* show their hole cards to their opponents. Why in the world would you want to share any information about your cards to your opponents? By showing your hole cards, you are letting them know the types of hands you play or don't play. Don't give them the satisfaction of increased awareness.

Of course, some opponents, especially the ones with big egos, are particularly susceptible to going on tilt when a successful bluff is revealed to them. If you think you can rattle a good player, or just set him or her up for a future move, it might be worth it. It's not showing off if you're making a calculated move to increase your win rate.

BANKROLL!

It's the last section of the chapter, but it's probably the most important.

Luck is a tremendous factor in poker. Yes, a skillful player will eventually come out on top. But it's not uncommon for even great players to have bad weeks, months, and in some cases, years. There's only one way to survive these runs of misfortune, and that's bankroll.

Bankroll is particularly important if you're dipping into the middle-limit waters for the first time, as the tables are full of moneyed maniacs who will put you to the test early and often. Make a few critical mistakes, suffer a poor run of cards and a bad beat or three, and a year's worth of low-limit winnings can be wiped out in a flash. There's nothing more worthless than luck turned positive *after* you've wiped out your poker bank account.

While there's no rule etched in stone as to what kind of bankroll you'll need to survive a higher limit game, a good rule of thumb is three to four hundred big bets. Five hundred is even safer. In other words, you'll want to have $10,000–$20,000 behind you if you're planning to turn the local $20/40 game into your office.

Don't lock yourself into playing a specific limit. Just because you've started playing $20/40 doesn't mean you should continue if things go badly for you. If, for whatever reason, you suffer losses that take you below a $15,000 bankroll, drop down to the $15/30 table. At $10,000, get your ass into a $10/20 game. Yes, this can be humiliating, but even if you're a better player than everyone else at the $20/40 table, your bankroll won't be able to withstand the perfectly normal fluctuations that you will experience at that level.

If, on the other hand, things go very well, you can think about moving up when you reach the next level. Achieve a bankroll of $30,000 and you may be ready for the $30/60 game. At $100,000, take a vacation—you've earned it—then consider the $100/200 game. Always remember that as the stakes go up, the competition gets harder. You may discover that you were a bigger winner at $20/40 than at $80/$160, even if you can beat both games. The $20/40 game is also likely to be a lot less stressful.

One last note about this advice: While many are quick to offer it, almost no one follows it. As a result, nearly every great poker player has, at point or another, gone broke. Sometimes more than once. There are former World Champions who once had enough money to wallpaper their mansions with $20 bills who today are not only penniless, but carrying more debt than some Third World countries.

Handle your bankroll like a professional. Playing too high is a sure way to end up back in the real world or begging from friends. Take a lesson from Nick "the Greek" Dandalos, who after so many years of gambling for millions died nearly penniless. He finished his career playing $5/10 draw in southern California, where a stranger reportedly asked him how he could play for such small stakes.

To which Dandalos famously replied, "Hey, it's action, isn't it?"

♥ ♦ ♣ ♠ ♥ ♦ ♣ ♠ ♥ ♦ ♣ ♠ ♥ ♦ ♣ ♠ ♥ ♦ ♣ ♠ ♥ ♦ ♣ ♠ ♥ ♦ ♣ ♠

YOUR DEFINING MOMENT

Winning at the low-limits has, for you, begun to feel like fishing with a net. Some of the little guys are going to slip through the holes, but you've caught enough of them by the end of the day to make the trip worthwhile.

The fish at the middle-limit tables are cleverer, but at this point, so are you. It's time to learn how to use a rod instead of a net.

Match each of the fish below with the techniques that are most likely to land them

Type of Fish	My hand selection will be ...	After the flop, my play will be ...	I will bluff ...
The Bluffer. Loves to Will play any two cards, raising and re-raising after the flop regardless of what he has.	(a) normal (b) tighter (c) looser	(a) normal (b) more aggressive than usual (c) more passive than usual	(a) as usual (b) more frequently (c) less frequently
The Callingfish. Doesn't like to raise before the flop, but once in, will call to the river with even the usual slimmest chances of winning.	(a) normal (b) tighter (c) looser	(a) normal (b) more aggressive than usual (c) more passive than usual	(a) as usual (b) more frequently (c) less frequently
The Rockfish. Plays very few hands, and most of the time, they're premium. Almost never bluffs, doesn't like to bet unless he's got the nuts or close to it.	(a) normal (b) tighter (c) looser	(a) normal (b) more aggressive than usual c) more passive than usual	(a) as usual (b) more frequently (c) less frequently

♥ ♦ ♣ ♠ ♥ ♦ ♣ ♠ ♥ ♦ ♣ ♠ ♥ ♦ ♣ ♠ ♥ ♦ ♣ ♠ ♥ ♦ ♣ ♠ ♥ ♦ ♣ ♠

THE ANSWERS

The Bluffer: (b) tighter hand selection, (c) more passive than usual after the flop, (a) bluff as usual.

The Bluffer is a lucrative fish, but will bite back if you're not patient. You're going to play fewer hands, focusing on premium hands like big pocket pairs and high suited connectors, throwing some small pairs into the mix—you want hands that will connect strongly with the flop. After the flop, you'll want to check and call more than usual. Don't let him have free cards, but don't bother getting into raising wars either, unless you're holding the nuts. Most of the time he'll bet your hand for you, and you'll save a few bets those times he spikes a miracle card to beat you. Many Bluffers are themselves susceptible to bluffs, especially if you're playing tight and have managed to showdown a few winners, but don't get carried away— some varieties of Bluffers are so afraid of being shown up that they'll call you to the end even if they're bluffing, on the off-chance that you're bluffing with something worse than they are.

The Callingfish: (a) normal hand selection, (b) more aggressive than usual after the flop, (c) bluff less frequently.

Callingfish make a great meal but need to be pummeled before you can drag them into the boat. Play your normal selection of hands. If you connect with the flop, however, you've got to punish that Callingfish for calling. Look for opportunities to confront him with double-bets, using positional raises and check-raises. He may call you anyway, and will win some big pots those times he sucks out on you, but if you play smart, you'll win a larger number of those big pots and come out ahead. It's almost entirely pointless to bluff a Callingfish, as they're not very good at folding.

The Rockfish. (c) looser hand selection, (a) normal after the flop, (b) bluff more frequently.

The Rockfish don't have a lot of meat to them—your more satisfying meals will come from other parts of the sea—but sometimes they're the only food around. You can play more hands against these fish because you'll have a much better sense of when the flop has missed *them* (i.e., almost any flop that doesn't have a picture card) and will be able to pick up pots with your bottom and middle pairs. Play as aggressively as you normally would after the flop, maybe even erring on the side of caution—the Rockfish will often check and call in a spot where you might have raised. They won't put a lot of tricky plays on you, so you can usually give them credit for a hand when they bet. When they don't, however, it's your invitation to bluff at the pot, especially if you've thrown them off-balance by showing down a few junk hands. You want them to think that you could be playing *anything*, so they'll be quick to throw away their hands when they fail to connect.

9

"THE CADILLAC OF POKER GAMES"

That's how Doyle Brunson describes no-limit Texas Hold'em in *Super/System.* It's also probably the main reason that poker has exploded like a five-megaton hydrogen bomb. No-limit is fast and furious, and it embodies all of the "old school" preconceived notions that people have when they think "poker."

No-limit Texas Hold'em is the game played on TV for millions of dollars. You've seen ESPN's broadcasts of the World Series of Poker, Bravo's *Celebrity Poker Showdown,* and of course, Travel Channel's World Poker Tour. Stone cold faces. Huge suckouts for huge pots. The big bluff. It's even added a unique phrase to the American lexicon—

"I'm all-in!"—an invitation for the audience to crane their necks to get a better look at the action, their hearts racing.

That's no-limit, the "Cadillac of Poker," and as Mike Sexton, the poker analyst on the World Poker Tour, is fond of saying, "It takes a minute to learn and a lifetime to master." It's a game that requires all of the skills you've developed at the limit tables, only in greater quantities: more patience, as some of the hands you've grown used to playing become less useful; more strategy, as you'll be able to manipulate the size of the pot; more bravery, because at any given moment, you may have to make a decision that will dictate the fate of your entire stack of chips.

BANKROLL

You may have grown up hearing stories about the poker games of the Wild West, where a player might risk his money, horse, or ranch on the turn of a card. In his book *Big Deal*, Anthony Holden tells the story of how, on her wedding night, Virgie Moss found herself standing behind her new husband Johnny as he played in a high-stakes game. When he found himself short of the chips he needed to stay in a particularly big hand, Johnny reached back and, without looking, tried to wrest the engagement ring from her hand. Perhaps realizing for the first time what kind of marriage she had gotten herself into, "Virgie disentangled herself from his grasp, removed the ring herself, and handed it over. 'If'n Ah hadn't,' she said, 'Johnny would've ripped mah whole finguh off.'"

Somewhere along the line the concept of "all-in" arose. A player could wager as much as he wanted, but his opponent could only be forced to risk whatever was in front of him. Let's say you have $5,000 in chips: Player A might bet $10,000, but you're only on the hook for what you have—$5,000. Of course, you can only win $5,000, but your horse and ranch are safe.

That doesn't make a decision to push all-in any easier. The player with the larger stack always has an advantage over the smaller stacks, as he can put his opponents "to the test," forcing them to decide whether or not it's worth risking all of their chips to see his cards. It's intense stuff.

So how big does your bankroll have to be? Sufficient to cover the stakes, whatever they might be, and preferably large enough to allow you to be the aggressor. And, as before, scared money is dead money, so bring enough for a rebuy if you get unlucky (or do something stupid) and go broke.

In cardrooms, no-limit games generally have a maximum buy-in, preventing the richest player at the table from totally steamrolling over the competition.

TIGHTEN UP

Making a successful transition from limit to no-limit poker will require a few subtle but incredibly important shifts in the way you've learned to think about poker. The first is in the way you value your hands.

Early in your limit poker career, you discovered that many of your decisions were made with an eye toward the long run. It was still profitable, for example, to miss a flush draw three or four times as long as, when you finally hit it, the pot was big enough to cover your previous failures.

The game was all about expected value.

No-limit poker also incorporates expected value, but with a twist—if you risk all your chips and miss, you're toast. It's a little bit like Russian Roulette, which would be a phenomenal game—you're a 5-to-1 favorite to win!—if only the penalty for losing weren't so cost-prohibitive.

In order to play Russian Roulette, a sane person would want to be assured, before pulling the trigger, that the chamber contained no bullet. Fortunately, no-limit poker occasionally offers that kind of assurance in the form of the nuts. You can always, just by glancing at a hold'em board, figure out what the best possible hand could be. And you can always, just by peeking at your cards, figure out if you've got it.

There's a much greater emphasis, therefore, on playing hands that will combine with the board to make unbeatable hands, or at least very powerful ones. Tight is right. There are a good many successful no-limit players who hate to play anything other than a Group One hand unless they're "advertising," hoping to make you believe they're the kind of player who will play something other than a Group One hand.

You don't want to play hands that can be dominated. Ace-jack, for example, is a strong hand, one that you'll often raise with in a limit game. It's not, however, the hand you want to be holding when you're being forced to risk all of your chips, as it's a big underdog against ace-king, ace-queen, or any big pocket pair—which just happen to be the kinds of hands that an opponent would push all-in with.

This isn't to say that you should never play A-J in a no-limit game. It's still a very strong hand, as long as you can avoid those situations where it's dominated. How do you know when your opponents have Group One hands? Well, they'll usually be raising.

You've got to take pre-flop raises very seriously in a no-limit game, especially if they come from early position. Calling raises is a dangerous business. Returning for one last morbid look at our Russian Roulette example, you'd much rather be the player pointing the gun than the one with the muzzle to your temple.

AN AGGRESSIVE MIND-SET

No-limit poker doesn't just reward aggression, it *requires* it. When it's your turn to act, consider running through the following script in your head:

What are some of the hands my opponents are likely to hold?

What do my opponents think I have?

Are my opponents playing conservatively? Aggressively? Tentatively?

Should I bet or raise?

Should I bet or raise?

Should I bet or raise?

If you answer no to the raise-raise-raise question . . .

Should I check or fold?

Should I check or fold?

Should I check or fold?

If you answer no to the fold-fold-fold questions, then, finally . . .

Should I call?

If you're in late position, and no one has raised in front of you, you can think about calling (or, even better, *raising*) with some weaker hands. The tricky part is knowing which weaker hands to play. For reasons that will become evident, those suited aces and connectors—drawing hands— that were such a profitable part of your limit game are going to have to be played very differently at the no-limit table. If you don't flop a made hand, you're usually going to be punished badly for chasing.

Playing small pocket pairs before the flop for a lot of chips is usually a very bad idea. If you get called, you're at best a very marginal favorite against two overcards, and you're at worst a 4.5-to-1 underdog against a higher pocket pair.*

They are, however, a great hand to play cheaply. When you flop trips, you're going to be in great position to trap your opponents. Players have a tendency to overplay their top pair-good kicker hands, and they'll be drawing almost

---

* Winding up with pocket pairs against two overcards is often called a "classic showdown." The pocket pairs are usually a *slight* favorite to win, but for all practical purposes, it's a flip of a coin.

completely dead to your set. If you don't hit your set on the flop, the hand is very easy to throw away and you've lost the minimum.

TRAPPING

When you flop a really, really big hand, it sometimes pays to "trap" your opponent and give them an opportunity to catch up a bit. You're hoping that if you wait until the turn or the river to bet, that your opponent may catch good enough cards to call a big bet, but not good enough cards to beat you.

For instance, let's say you have pocket jacks in the small blind. A middle-position tight player raises and you decide to just call and see the flop. The flop comes J-J-4. You have flopped four of a kind, and your hand is virtually unbeatable. Now, if you bet right out, you will probably not win a single dollar more. Let's say your opponent has A-K. After you bet, he's probably going to fold! But if you check and an ace or a king comes on the turn, you might just break the poor guy. You check and hope, and pray, that the guy catches up a bit on the turn so that you can make some more money. Now, if the turn comes a 6 or something similar, you might even choose to trap again and give him another chance to catch up on the river.

Understand that by trapping with hands that are less than a complete lock, you are often giving your opponents a chance to draw cards that will beat you. The ideal hands to trap with have three different suits on the flop and the cards are well spread apart. For example, 10-7-2 with three different suits after you flop a set of tens is a good flop to slowplay, whereas J-9-8 with two spades on the board is not a good hand to slowplay if you flop a set.

Slowplaying or trapping has greater value against aggressive players who will bluff at a pot than it does against passive players who always bet and raise based on the value of their hand. Simply put, passive players won't bet weak hands for you, and they are unlikely to call bets with weak hands. Slowplaying has very little value against these types of players—you'll have to beat them with pure aggression.

CONTROLLING THE SIZE OF THE POT

Many of your decisions at the limit tables were dictated by the size of the pot. Flop four cards to a flush, or an open-ended straight draw, and you were almost always getting the right odds to call a bet or two in the hopes of completing your hand.

It's a logic that probably frustrated you at times. Flopping a set, for example, can be very aggravating when there are two (or three) cards of the same suit on the board. You know that someone is going to be chasing a hand that can beat yours and—what's worse—they're correct in doing so.

In no-limit, you get to be the man (or woman) behind the curtain, pulling the strings. You can use the size of your bets to control the pot odds your opponent is receiving.

Say, for example, you're playing $10/20 limit hold'em and are dealt [A♦] [A♣] . You raise before the flop, scaring off everyone except the woman in the small blind, who calls you with J♦ 10♥ . Two players, $40 in the pot and the flop comes

K♥ 7♠ 2♥ .

You're obviously in front, but you'll be beaten by any heart, giving your opponent nine outs. Going back to the *rule of four,* she's got about a 36 percent chance of winning the hand by the river, or pot odds of about 2-to-1. Given that there's already $40 in the pot—$50 after you bet your hand—she'll be getting 5-to-1 odds to call, and would be correct to do so. You're going to bet your hand to the river, praying that the third heart doesn't fall.

Now let's take the same situation in no-limit hold'em. What if, instead of betting $10 after the flop, you were to bet $100? There would be $140 in the pot, but it would cost her $100 to call, giving her pot odds of 1.4-to-1. A call here would be incorrect, leading a smart opponent to lay down her hand, and a not-so-smart one to make an unprofitable decision.

Being able to control the size of the pot is an awesome power, which, as is the case with so many awesome powers, comes with the ability to hang oneself. In no-limit hold'em, this is often accomplished by **overbetting** or **underbetting** the pot.

You're overbetting the pot when you risk a large amount of money to win a little. The classic example is moving all-in when you're sitting on a medium to large stack. You'll win a relatively small amount—the pot—those times you win, but will lose everything those times you don't. Players who overbet the pot are generally doing so in the hopes that they won't be called.

178 POKER

Underbetting, on the other hand, occurs when you bet a small amount into a large pot. For example, if there is $5,000 in the pot, it would be silly to bet $100, as you'd be giving your opponents the right odds to call you with nearly anything.

Many experienced no-limit players like to make most of their bets and raises the size of the pot. The consistency helps to conceal the true strength of their hands, while the size of the bet makes it incorrect for their opponents to pursue most of their draws.

As a result, suited aces and connectors—your bread and butter at the limit tables—lose some of their value in a no-limit game, as skilled players will make bets large enough to keep you from pursuing your straight and flush draws. By the same token, small and medium pocket pairs can be your best friends, especially if you can play them cheaply. You'll either flop a set, putting you in the driver's seat, or you won't, making it easy to lay the hand down should you face any threatening action.

HEART

In *Positively Fifth Street,* writer Jim McManus's account of his experience at the 2000 World Series of Poker, he describes the moment when he decides to call an all-in bet against his poker hero, the legendary T. J. Cloutier, with just an ace high. "Ah'd bet on that boy," Amarillo Slim Preston observed. "He's got the heart of a cliff divah."

When partaking in the Cadillac of poker games, strategy will take you only so far. Eventually you will have to make a decision for all of your chips. The ability to not just function, but excel, in the face of this kind of pressure is what separates the great no-limit players from the merely good.

Risking all of your chips in the absence of anything but the nuts requires courage. Recovering from suckouts or bad beats that can, in the literal sense of the word, decimate your stack takes intestinal fortitude. Being able to bluff an opponent into laying down a better hand often depends on superior calm and composure.

There are many mathematically proficient players who excel at the limit game but don't have what it takes to succeed when those limits are erased. Maybe British novelist and poet Rudyard Kipling put it best when he said,

> If you can make one heap of all your winnings
> And risk it all on one turn of pitch-and-toss,
> And lose, and start again at your beginnings
> And never breathe a word about your loss;
> If you can force your heart and nerve and sinew
> To serve your turn long after they are gone,
> And so hold on when there is nothing in you
> Except the Will which says to them: "Hold on!"
> . . . . Yours is the Earth and everything that's in it,
> And—which is more—you'll be a Man, my son!

♥ ♦ ♣ ♠ ♥ ♦ ♣ ♠ ♥ ♦ ♣ ♠ ♥ ♦ ♣ ♠ ♥ ♦ ♣ ♠ ♥ ♦ ♣ ♠

YOUR DEFINING MOMENT

The local casino has recently begun spreading a $200 maximum buy-in, $1/2 blind no-limit game. You've got plenty of bankroll for the trip, and your solid play of late has you feeling good. You start feeling even better as you

approach the table—there's your buddy Perry, easily one
of the worst players in your regular home game, sitting
behind a stack of what must be a thousand $1 chips. He's
beating this game like a redheaded stepchild. You take the
only empty seat, on Perry's right.

Perry's in the middle of a big pot. The Rock he's playing
against isn't the type to give any action without the nuts or
near to it—Perry's obviously drawing against a made hand.
That doesn't stop Perry, who calls a $60 all-in bet, turns over
his gut-shot straight draw and says, "I think I need help."
The Rock agrees, flipping over the top set, but POW! The
river brings Perry's miracle straight card. "REBUY!"
screams the Rock, as Perry makes an obnoxious Incredible
Hulk pose before dragging in the monster pot.

You buy the maximum $200 in chips and post the big
blind, where, on your very first hand, you discover
A♠ K♠ . Perry makes it $10 from under the gun, two
players call and the action's on you. You think of a number
to raise—with $33 already in the pot, $35 seems about
right—and pop it. Perry looks at you with disdain and
calls quickly. The others fold. You're heads-up against your
buddy, $103 in the pot.

The flop comes 8♦ 5♣ 2♣ , not exactly what you
were hoping for. It's your turn—your Defining Moment—but
before you can act, Perry's mountain of chips comes tum-
bling down, hits his cards, and accidentally tips up the
7♠ . He covers it quickly, but he knows that you saw the
card.

What do you do?

♥ ♦ ♣ ♠ ♥ ♦ ♣ ♠ ♥ ♦ ♣ ♠ ♥ ♦ ♣ ♠ ♥ ♦ ♣ ♠ ♥ ♦ ♣ ♠

THE ANSWER

You run through your mental script:

What are some of the hands my opponents are likely to hold?

Pocket 7s, 7♠ 6♠, 8♠ 7♠, maybe 9♠ 7♠ or 7♠ 5♠ or 7♠ 4♠. The wired sevens seem most likely, as he'd probably lay down any of the other hands in the face of your raise.

What do my opponents think I have?

Perry knows my game well enough to know that I'd need a very good hand to raise out of position: a big pair, A-K, maybe A-Q.

Are my opponents playing conservatively? Aggressively? Tentatively?

He's playing like a maniac!

Should I bet or raise?

Assuming he has one of the hands above, he's likely to call any kind of medium-sized bet. Against 7-7, 8-7, or 7-5 you have about a 25 percent chance of winning. Against 7-6, it's about 50-50. If he's got 9-7, you are about a 70 percent favorite.

Let's say you bet something like $50, and he moves you all-in (for your remaining $105) with 7-7. You would *have* to call, as the $400 or so in the pot gives you the proper odds to call with your 25 percent chance of winning. (You would be **pot committed,** a concept that's discussed in more detail in the next chapter.) Betting any less would be pointless, as Perry would have the odds to call with all kinds of draws.

Should I check or fold?

How about a check, with the intention of check-raising all-in? That seems very strong; it *might* get him to lay down 7-7, although, depending on the size of his bet, he'd probably have the right odds to call your all-in with 8-7 or 7-5. If he's on a drawing hand, however, your check-raise seems to be the right thing to do.

So you check. He shoots you a quick, nasty smile and checks behind you. What is that? A good play, that's what. He obviously put you on A-K, while he's obviously on a draw. You're guessing 7♠ 6♠ —if he only had a gut-shot, he probably would have tried to steal the pot with an all-in bet, representing pocket sevens.

You hold your breath as the turn comes, but it's a beautiful K♦. Your bet.

Okay, you're clearly ahead here. If he does in fact have 7♠ 6♠ , he's drawing to eight cards, the four nines and the four fours. With one card to come, Perry has about a 16 percent chance of making his straight on the river. You might be tempted to move all-in here, taking down the $103 that's already in the pot. Not such a bad play. But now that you're in the driver's seat, why not give Perry a chance to make an even bigger mistake?

Let's say you bet $20, bringing the pot up to $133. Twenty dollars is about 15 percent of $133, meaning Perry would (more or less) have the correct odds to call. Bet less than $20, and he has to call. To call a bet over $20, however, would be a mistake—and you're the beneficiary. Judging by his current feeling of invincibility, you figure you can get him to call a $40 or $50 bet. Remember, you *want* him to call on the turn, as long as his call is more than $20.

So you settle on a $45 bet. He calls instantly. Sweet! Until, of course, the river hits and it's the dreaded 9. "Wow, what a river card," he says before you can even process what has happened. You check, he bets all-in, and you fold quickly. He doesn't torture you by showing a bluff—he turns up the made straight. You shrug your shoulders, open your wallet, and call for a rebuy. Perry won this one, but you know that you'll come out ahead if you keep making great analyses like this one.

10

THE FINAL TABLE

In 1970, when Johnny Moss was declared winner of the first World Series of Poker, he was indebted to his fellow players in the most straightforward way imaginable: He was elected by popular vote.

According to 1972 champion Amarillo Slim Preston, the tournament's current format is due in good part to the comments of Ted Thackery, a reporter for the *Los Angeles Times* who had traveled to Las Vegas to cover the event. "You gotta find some way to make it a contest," observed the reporter. "If you want to get the press involved and turn the World Series into a real sporting event, you need to give it some structure, create some drama, and make it like a real tournament."

"Freeze-out!" suggested Slim. The champion would be the player who won—and got to keep—everyone else's entry money. And so poker's greatest tournament was born.

Aside from the competitive drama, tournaments provide their players with something even more significant, at least to the poker mind: an **overlay.** An entrant can risk a relatively small amount of money to win a substantially larger amount. Those familiar with the Chris Moneymaker story know that the road to his $2.5 million payday began with a $40 entry fee in an online **supersatellite.**

Gamblers of all stripes love overlays—witness the popularity of the Powerball Lottery. Unlike the lottery, which sophisticated bettors know to be a terrible wager in terms of expected value—poker tournaments are a boon to skilled rounders thanks to **dead money,** the field of weaker opponents who, in the eyes of the pros, have little to no chance of winning. (Of course, Chris Moneymaker was considered by many to be dead money pretty much up until the moment he won.)

TOURNAMENTS VS. RING GAMES

If you're a fan of watching poker on TV, you've probably seen players like Gus Hansen or Phil Ivey rake in huge pots with all kinds of junk hands that you'd never consider playing in an everyday ring game. You might be tempted to think that, when it comes to poker tournaments, all of the rules are tossed out the window.

You'd be forgetting that televised poker, like other programmed entertainment, is edited for your viewing pleasure. For every brilliant display of bluster or cunning, there are a dozen or so "boring" hands, like everyone folding to the blinds or a small raise that scares everybody off.

Winning tournaments depends in large part on the same set of skills required to win ring games: tight, aggressive play, making accurate reads and decisions. The distinction between the two is, in a weird way, metaphysical.

You should play ring games as if you're going to live forever. Every decision gets graded against "the long run," or, in statistical terms, infinity. It's okay to push when you've got even the slightest edge and to make your share of marginal calls, as these mathematically correct decisions will, over time, show a profit.

Tournaments are all about mortality, a beginning and an end. One wrong play and you're dead. Even if every decision you make is correct, you are still beholden to the tournament's finite lifespan. A cold run of cards in the face of increasing blinds and antes can be just as devastating as your worst mistake. Luck plays a big role in tournaments, which is why a few previously unknown amateurs are wearing gold bracelets, while some of the all-time greats are still looking for their first World Series title.

THE ANATOMY OF A TOURNAMENT

It all begins with a buy-in. The number of chips you begin with is particular to each tournament. In some cases—the World Series, for one—there's a one-to-one relationship between the buy-in and your starting stack, i.e., the $10,000 entry fee will provide you with $10,000 in chips.* It's more common, however, to start with a stack that's

---

* Lest you think casinos host these tournaments out of the goodness of their hearts, there's a hidden cost here as well in the form of "tournament fees." Nearly $700 of the vaunted $10,000 entry fee to the WSOP, for example, is deducted from the prize pool for the casino's coffers.

significantly larger than your buy-in: A $20 tournament wouldn't be very interesting or last very long if each player had only $20 to toss around.

Unlike a ring game, where there's nothing to prevent you from reaching into your pocket to replenish your supply of chips, your starting tournament stack is your lifeline. Lose it and you're done. (The obvious exception would be a tournament with **rebuys** or **add-ons,** concepts we'll come back to a little later.)

As if that weren't enough pressure, most tournaments are broken down into smaller blocks of time called levels. With each new level comes an increase in the blinds, limits, and, in some cases, antes. That $10,000 starting stack might seem like a small fortune when the blinds are $25 and $50. But if you haven't significantly improved your position by Day Three, when the $800-$1,600 blinds have been supplemented by a $200 ante, you're going to find yourself in serious trouble.

THE TRAIL OF TEARS

When you're sitting on a short stack, watching the tournament clock as it ticks down toward the next increase in blinds and antes can fill you with an undeniable sense of dread. If you happen to be playing in the World Series—or an increasing number of other tournaments that have adopted the TEARS format—you can thank Tex Morgan for this particular act of cruelty.

Increase the blinds and limits too quickly, and you force players into early wild action. Too slow, and you'll have a tournament that drags on for days. These inconsistencies led Morgan, a former rodeo rider and competitive archer, to develop TEARS (or Tournament Evaluation and Rating System). "I have had very little math training," Morgan readily admits. "However, I am a problem solver. I knew what the problem was for years and I figured out a way to solve it."

A freely distributed computer program, TEARS customizes the length of a tournament's levels to best suit the number of entrants and the chips in play. Proponents of the system argue that it creates a saner environment for good players, who can afford to be more patient during the early stages of a tournament. Critics believe that it takes too long to winnow down the field, forcing players into too many life-or-death situations in the later stages.

TYPES OF TOURNAMENTS

Tournaments come in all flavors. Some online cardrooms offer half-table tournaments with $2.50 entry fees that are over in less than half an hour. At the other end of the spectrum, more than twenty-five hundred people are expected to participate in the 2004 World Series, each ponying up $10,000 in the hopes of surviving seven grueling fourteen-hour days.

SIT & GOS

The concept is deceptively simple: a single-table tournament that begins as soon as a sufficient number of players, generally five or ten, have gathered. Okay, there's nothing deceptive about it; it's just simple.

Sit & Gos first became popular as satellites for larger tournaments. In the weeks, days, and hours preceding big-time events with substantial buy-ins, you'll see players competing in these single-table contests, hoping to earn a seat on the cheap. Maybe you don't have $10,000 to enter the World Series, but you might consider plopping down $1,000 to compete against nine other players for a chance to play in the main event.

They're also extremely popular in online cardrooms. You add your name to a waiting list, and as soon as enough players have gathered, the tournament begins. Unlike satellites, the online Sit & Gos usually pay the top three places, meaning that as long as you can beat seven other players (or two, in a five-person tournament) you'll at least win back your entry fee.

Sit & Gos are designed to be played quickly and usually feature a rapidly increasing blind and ante structure to force players into action. There are two basic—and very different—strategies for winning:

(1) **Amass chips early and often.** A lot of players will start the tournament with guns blazing, entering pots with all kinds of hands in the hopes of building a huge stack before the blinds get nasty—or getting knocked out quickly enough to sign up for another Sit & Go. You'll be eliminated early more times than not, but it can be a reasonably effective strategy if you plan on entering a few satellites in the hopes of winning a more expensive seat.

It's a terrible way to play in a single-table tournament that pays second and third place finishers, as the first prize won't be large enough to compensate for all of the times you make an early exit. Your emphasis in these types of Sit & Gos should be finishing in the money.

(2) **Lay in wait.** Unless you've been lucky enough to amass a disproportionately large number of chips in the early going, the middle rounds—when the blinds and antes represent a substantial portion of your stack—are going to be tough going. Many players like to avoid getting into confrontations in the early going, waiting for a spot to go all-in in the middle and later stages of the tournament. It's a somewhat safer strategy than the previous one, especially if you're looking to survive into the money, but it comes with its own set of risks. You may not get dealt a premium hand in the middle rounds and get killed by the blinds and antes. Even if you do manage to double-up, it may not be enough to compete against an early-round gambler who is already sitting on a mountain of chips.

There's no best way to win a single-table tournament. Even the most cunning strategist is helpless in the face of an ice-cold run of cards or someone else's idiotic good fortune. In the end, it often comes down to making good reads, picking your spots . . . and getting lucky.

SQUIRM TIME

You'll see the same performance by almost every professional on the World Poker Tour when it's his or her turn to act. They'll stare their opponent down, stacking and restacking their chips. They might make vague allusions to the strength of their own hand, then ask questions like, "How much do you have left?" or "How deep are you?"

It's Squirm Time. The prods and the pauses are calculated efforts to get an opposing player to slip up, revealing some vital piece of information about his or her cards.

Squirm time has the added virtue of allowing you a breather before committing to an action. A poker player must be, at times, a police detective, examining a suspect's story—everything he or she has done up to this point in the hand—from all angles, looking for inconsistencies or other bits of weirdness that might provide a clue to the truth of the matter. Great poker decisions are rarely made quickly. As they say in high school Driver's Ed, speed kills.

MULTI-TABLE TOURNAMENTS

Sit & Go tournaments make for good practice, but it's incredibly unlikely that you'll ever get rich playing them. Poker's biggest prizes are earned by surviving extended battles against hundreds of opponents.

Not all multi-table tournaments are created equal. Some, especially those with smaller entry fees, have rapidly accelerating blinds and antes, forcing players to make the same kind of all-or-nothing decisions prevalent in the single-table tournaments. Others, like the events you'll see on the World Poker Tour, can last for days, enabling participants to play a more subtle and patient game.

A lot of smaller tournaments offer add-ons and rebuys during their first stage. As the names suggest, add-ons are extra tournament chips that can be purchased with "real" money, while rebuys give players who have busted out the opportunity to purchase a second chance. The upside is in the prize pool—players often average three or four rebuys in these kinds of tournaments, which in turn triple or quadruple the amount of money available to win. The downside is that the first stage is often dominated by wild play, as risk-takers can get mixed up in all kinds of gambles knowing that a new lease on life is just a matter of reaching back into the wallet.

Daniel Negreanu, one of the best players in the world, entered the 2004 World Series of Poker $1,000 buy-in no-limit tournament—an event that allows rebuys—on a mission. After only two hours, he had made twenty-seven rebuys! In other words, his entry fee into the tournament was $27,000. To have any hope to recouping his investment, he had to finish no worse than eighth, no easy feat given a field of around 800 players. As it turned out, Daniel clearly knew what he was doing. He finished third—good for over $80,000—and made a tidy $53,000 profit.

Whether you love or hate these kinds of tournaments depends in large part on your bankroll. If you can afford to keep pace with the maniacs yelling "rebuy!" every five minutes (maybe even engaging in a little of this lunacy yourself) and aren't afraid to max out your add-ons, you can often build a substantial stack before the first break, putting you in strong position to make a go at the expanded prize pool. If merely entering the tournament means skipping lunches for a year, you're going to be at a distinct disadvantage against those players who are willing and able to replenish their chip supply.

There are no add-ons or rebuys in the World Series of Poker championship event or any World Poker Tour event.

CHOOSING A TOURNAMENT

Professionals generally choose tournaments based on two criteria: (a) the potential payday, and (b) the likelihood that they're going to be able to outplay a substantial portion of the field. Nearly any tournament where you're better than half your opponents represents a good investment.

When you're just starting out, your options may be a little more limited. If you're lucky enough to live near a card-room, there are probably daily or weekly tournaments for you to take advantage of, with $10 to $20 buy-ins. These tend to be spirited, even wild games, especially when there are rebuys, add-ons, and alcohol, but they provide invaluable experience at a relatively inexpensive price.

Almost every major cardroom holds at least one big tournament during the year. Many of these tournaments are preceded by a week or so of warm-ups, with entry fees of $300 or so, competitive contests that will often attract players you've seen on TV. If the $300 seems like a lot to risk against serious competition, you might find that you can win your way in via a single-table satellite earlier in the day.

If you don't live near a cardroom, you may be able to find a privately held tournament near you via a Web site like *www.homepokergames.com*.

There are plenty of tournaments online as well, some of which can be very lucrative. Many sites (including

FullTiltPoker.com) offer "freerolls" to their regular customers, one of life's rare opportunities to win something
for nothing. The more popular sites offer numerous
opportunities to play your way into major events like the
WSOP or WPT Finals.

If you're an excellent reader of personalities or physical
tells, you'll be giving up a bit of an edge playing against
cyber-opponents. Then again, Chris Moneymaker, the
most famous online tournament winner of all time, hadn't
ever set foot in a brick-and-mortar, real-life cardroom
before the 2003 WSOP.

TOURNAMENT STRUCTURE: AN EXAMPLE

Here's a sample structure from a recent hold'em tournament held at Foxwoods Casino:

$15 BUY-IN—$5 ENTRY FEE

One $10 optional rebuy for $1,000 in tournament chips
All players start with $1,000 in tournament chips

LEVEL	SMALL BLIND	LARGE BLIND	LIMIT
1	$15	$25	$25-50
	*Color Up and Race for $5 Chips**		
2	$25	$50	$50-$100
3	$50	$75	$75-$150
4	$75	$100	$100-$200

* As the size of the blinds increases, chips of lower denominations are taken out
of play by "coloring up" to the next denomination. Players then "race" for the
odd chips. In this example, the $5 chips (which, in this particular tournament,
are red) are taken out of play at the end of the first round. If you had six red
chips, you would color up five for one $25 (green) chip. The dealer would then
deal one card to each player for every leftover chip. The player with the highest
card wins the odd chips, which are converted to the next denomination (in this
case, a green chip). This process is repeated as the tournament progresses.

10-Minute Break			
5	$100	$200	$200-$400
6	$150	$300	$300-$600
	Color Up and Race for $25 Chips		
7	$200	$500	$500-$1,000
	Color Up and Race for $100 Chips		
8	$500	$1,000	$1,000-$2,000
10-Minute Break			
9	$1,000	$1,500	$1,500-$3,000
10	$1,500	$3,000	$3,000-$6,000
11	$2,500	$5,000	$5,000-$10,000
12	$5,000	$10,000	$10,000-$20,000
13	$10,000	$20,000	$20,000-$30,000
14	$15,000	$30,000	$30,000-$60,000
Each level is 20 minutes long			

WINNING YOUR FIRST TOURNAMENT
IN THE BEGINNING . . .

You've ponied up your entry fee in exchange for a plastic card with two numbers on it: your table and your seat. Your pile of chips is waiting for you. You settle into a comfortable position.

As the old saying goes, you never get a second chance at a first impression (at least until your table gets reshuffled—more on that later). You are going to be studying your opponents; they will be studying you. So what kind of image do you want to project?

There are a few incredibly good tournament players who like to come out firing, participating in more than their fair share of pots, hoping to amass a large stack of chips early. It can be a devastatingly effective strategy: Not only can these players win a lot of chips when their junk hands make unlikely connections with the board, but their opponents are going to have to pay them off those times when they actually hold a real hand. While they risk busting out early of a few more tournaments than their more conservative counterparts, it's a chance they consider worth taking.

If this kind of loose, aggressive play suits your personality, then by all means pursue it. Be forewarned, however, that unless you are a world-class reader of opponents and have a sixth sense for danger and a natural propensity toward luck, it's very difficult way to be a consistent winner.

Alternatively, you could, upon sitting down, decide to play the tightest poker you've ever played during the first two levels of the tournament. A few reasons why this isn't such a bad idea:

You probably won't get busted out. You raise with A-J from early position and get called by a player in late position. The flop comes A-10-5. You make a healthy, pot-sized bet. Your opponent considers for a minute, then pushes all-in. What do you do?

Well, you almost have to fold, but the better question is why in hell you were playing A-J from early position in the beginning stages of a no-limit tournament.

While they're all decent plays in your regular limit play, hands like A-Q, A-J, and K-Qs can all be thrown away unless you're in great position to play them (i.e., being the first to enter an unraised pot somewhere near the button). Maybe you'll limp in with a hand like J-10 or 8-7s in late position, but there's got to be a good reason for doing so—remember that it's very difficult to play drawing hands in no-limit poker. Smart players will punish you for chasing straights or flushes. Even when you flop your hand—say you're holding 10♥ 9♥ and the board delivers three hearts—can you call an all-in bet? A fourth heart (which will arrive on the turn or the river about one in every three times) and you may be done.

So what can you play? Obviously hands like A-A, A-K, and K-K are worth entering the pot with a raise. Just be prepared to ditch them if you run into suspicious action after the flop. Early in a tournament, it's almost never worth calling an all-in bet with only one pair, even if it's an overpair to the board.

When you raise before the flop, try to make it the same amount every time, or you risk giving away information about the strength of your hand. A table will usually settle into a "standard raise" somewhere between $2\frac{1}{2}$ and $3\frac{1}{2}$ times the size of the big blind. There's nothing wrong with adhering to the custom.

Your best friend during the early rounds of the tournament may be the pocket pair. About one in every eight times, you're going to flop a set (or better) and have a really good chance of busting out an opponent or two. If the flop misses you, it's easy to eject yourself from the hand.

While flushes and straights have to announce themselves—everyone's wary when there's three suited or connected cards on the board—flopped sets are no-limit's silent assassins. Not only are they safely hidden from view, but any opponent foolish enough to call you will likely be drawing to a slim number of outs. If you're holding 8-8 against someone with A-K, and the board comes A-8-3, you're almost certainly going to be **doubling up.**

As you're getting 7-to-1 odds to flop three of a kind, it's generally worth playing pocket pairs at any time if it is relatively cheap to do so.

Winning isn't worth as much. Unless you're lucky enough to get someone all-in, the pots in the early going usually won't be large enough to have a huge impact on your tournament. You could sit out every hand during the first two levels (paying only the blinds), steal two or three blinds in the third level, and find yourself about where you started the day.

Living testimony: Phil Hellmuth Jr., who won it all in 1989, often arrives late—up to an hour or more—for the start of the World Series Championship event. Whether or not he is doing it for psychological reasons, because he's busy meditating in front of the mirror, or because he just loves to make an "entrance" has not yet (nor may ever be) determined.

You'll get more time to observe your opponents. Think of the first two levels of the tournament as a scouting opportunity. Sitting out of most of the hands will give you plenty of time to observe your opponents' strengths and weaknesses, tells, and betting patterns. Form a mental dossier on each player:

- Do they play too many hands? Too few? Do they play certain hands out of position?
- Do they seem intimidated? Overly aggressive?
- Are they consistent in the size of their raises, or is there some information to be gleaned from the amount that they bet?
- How aggressively do they try to steal their opponents'

blinds? How aggressively do they defend their own?

- How do they play after the flop? Will they chase draws? Do they have a tendency to overbet or underbet the pot?
- Do they have any physical tells?
- How often do they bluff?
- Are they willing to call huge bets with only one pair? Are they capable of laying a big pair down?

Your image will be tight. Remember that while you're busy watching everyone else, most of them will be keeping an eye on you. If you play your cards right (cough, cough), they will come to see you as the paradigm of tight play who won't contest a hand unless you've got the goods. You may get lucky and win a decent pot with a hand like 9-4 offsuit, but the harm you do to your table image may end up costing you in the long run.

You will find that having a tight image becomes extremely helpful when, come the third and fourth rounds, you completely alter your style of play.

CHANGING GEARS

When Herbert Yardley wrote *Education of a Poker Player* in 1957, he encouraged his readers to play a tight, conservative game, taking advantage of the fact that few opponents would be familiar with the odds.

By the time Doyle Brunson published *Super/System* twenty years later, most of his competitors were hip to the idea that they shouldn't be drawing for inside straights. What Texas Dolly cleverly realized, however, was that these tight, conservative players could be "encouraged" into mucking their less-than-nut hands through aggressive raising. Much of his chapter on no-limit hold'em is dedicated to his love of the semi-bluff with all of his chips.

Well, everyone's read that book, too. In today's tournaments, competitors need to be, possibly above all else, unpredictable. Poker players call it "changing gears."

Howard Lederer, who has won multiple tournaments on the World Poker Tour, once said of fellow star Phil Ivey: "He's capable of playing any two cards as if they were aces." It's very, very difficult to play against someone who plays unpredictably.

If you've been playing tight for the first couple of rounds, it's time to loosen up.* Your goal during the middle rounds should be to win all of the pots that you are "supposed" to win . . . plus a few that you shouldn't!

This doesn't mean yelling, "Hand selection be damned!" and mixing it up with whatever two cards you happen to be dealt.

The first couple of stages were all about staying out of pots unless you had the chance to make a huge score. You'll be doing the same thing in the middle rounds, but you'll be looking to scoop up a few smaller pots as well. The easiest way to do this is by stealing blinds.

As stated earlier, the pots in the early going tend to be too small to be worth contesting. In the middle stages, however, the increase in the size of the blinds—and, in many cases, the addition of antes—means there's more money in the middle before the cards are even dealt. And you are going to take some of it.

By this time you should have solid reads on at least a

---

* Of course, if you've found yourself involved in more pots than usual in the early going, it might be time to do exactly the opposite.

few of your opponents. You know which ones are most likely to fold their blinds to a raise. So raise them! It doesn't matter what you have—thanks to the tight image you've worked so hard to develop, they are going to have to give your bet some respect, hopefully more than it's due.

Steals work best when made from middle to late position. It's almost customary for the button to try and steal the blinds if no one has yet entered the pot; even your less shrewd opponents will be anticipating such a move. A raise from a slightly earlier position, however, tends to engender a little more respect.

Even if some of these raises get called by stalwart blinds, you'll have the advantage of getting to act last after the flop. By now you should know how they like to play when they've made some kind of hand—Do they bet? Check-raise?—and if they don't, you'll get another chance to bet at and possibly steal the pot.

But wait, that's not all . . . you're also going to know which larcenous players are most likely to attempt to steal *your* blinds. When they do, you can re-raise them. If you've caught them with their hand in the cookie jar, they're going to have to fold. If they have a legitimate hand, hopefully you can escape without much more than a nick.

It's easiest to steal from players who have an average-sized stack. Players who are short on chips will start to feel desperate and increasingly inclined to risk everything on a less-than-premium hand. Avoid these kinds of confrontations—even if you're a 2-to-1 favorite to beat them, there's no reason to expose yourself to this kind of risk at this point in the tournament. Much of the value in raising comes from the chance you'll win the blinds without having to see a flop, value that's lost when you are up against a small stack that's likely to call with just about any two cards.

On the flip side are the players who are sitting on large stacks. They're more likely to "play back at you" with the knowledge that, at any moment, they can force you into a decision concerning all of your chips.

That leaves the average guy, who is in the position of being able to throw away a hand without worrying too much about it (while perhaps harboring some fear of losing a sizeable pot and slipping below the mean). How do you determine what an "average-sized" stack looks like? Just divide the total number of chips in the tournament by the number of players remaining.

SIGNIFICANT CHANGES

Tournaments are full of "significant changes" that can alter the dynamics of a table, maybe just for the next hand or two, perhaps in a way that isn't readily apparent for an hour, or a day. When a significant change takes place, it's good practice to take a mental time-out to ponder its possible effects.

So what constitutes a significant change? Here are a few:

- A player goes broke.
- A player doubles up.
- A player gets caught bluffing.
- The blinds just doubled.
- You just lost a significant pot.

- You just won a significant pot.

In each case, you want to consider how the table dynamics have been altered, asking yourself questions like:

- Will I need to be more passive? Aggressive?
- Will the player who got caught bluffing be likely to bluff again in the next few hands?
- Do I need to change gears because of the new situation?

APPROACHING THE BUBBLE

By now the opportunities to pick up small pots should be abundantly clear. While there's a lot of "maneuvering" during the early rounds of a tournament, many of your opponents will display recognizable tendencies that you, the observant poker superstar, will be able to exploit.

As the middle rounds continue, you should look to steadily increase the size of your stack while exposing yourself to the minimum amount of risk. Pick up the equivalent of one or two blinds every time the button makes an orbit, and you can virtually stroll to the final table. If you're doing a good job of identifying steal opportunities, you only have to win three out of every four or five stabs at the pot, including the times you actually *have* a real hand.

The next great shift in tournament dynamics comes as the specter of the **Bubble** begins to loom large.

In the 2003 World Series, George Rechnitzer of Beverly Hills finished sixty-third and was rewarded for his efforts with a $15,000 payday.

John Strzemp, who at the final table in 1997 took a bad

beat from Stuey Ungar to finish second, took another bad beat in 2003 to finish sixty-fourth and got nothing.

The Bubble is that dramatic period in the tournament when the prize money becomes palpable. Many players are just trying to hang onto their chips, hoping to outlast the one or two unfortunate souls who will finish out of the money.

This is a good time to run roughshod over your opponents. You'll still be concentrating on the average stacks — the very big and very small stacks remain dangerous — but your pre-flop raises will become even more relentless.

It's extremely difficult to overcome one's natural instinct for survival, but if you can, the Bubble can be a great time to improve your position. The 2001 World Series paid prize money to its top forty-five finishers. With forty-seven players left, I had about $95,000 in chips. Over the next hour and a half—the time it took to eliminate those last two pesky hangers-on—I added around $100,000 to my stack as I won about 80 percent of the hands I played, never *once* having to show a hand down. By the time we cleared the Bubble, my $195,000 was the tenth largest stack in the tournament.

WHEN YOU HAVE A SHORT-STACK . . .

. . . it's important not to wait *too* long before looking to double up. If you move all-in with a paltry number of chips, you'll have opponents lining up to call you, figuring the benefits of eliminating you from the tournament outweigh whatever minimal hit they'll take should they lose.

Being short-stacked comes in three basic flavors.

- When you have 13-15 times the size of the big blind, look for opportunities to raise all-in against a loose raiser with an average or slightly above-average stack. If you can get him to fold, you'll usually pick up a pot around the size of five big blinds.

- When you have 9-11 times the size of the big blind, you have to start taking some significant risks. Re-raise all-in with any premium hand. Raise all-in to steal blinds from average or medium-big stacks.

- Once you get down to 4-6 times the big blind, you have only one move, and that move is all-in. If someone bets in front of you, you may have to call all-in with any pocket pair, an ace with a decent kicker, or any other hand that you think you have about a 50/50 chance of winning.

Never give up, even if you're down to your last chip. Jack "Treetop" Straus, at one point down to his last $500 chip, came back to win the 1982 World Series of Poker. More recently, in one of the first tournaments I played after turning pro, I found myself at the final table of a $500 buy-in no-limit tournament with an average stack. The very first hand at the final table, I played like a chump against another average stack and ended up with $100 left.

I anted up, got four-way action, and won. The next hand, I went all-in with my $400, once again found three players to stay with me and won $1,600. I folded a few bad hands before finding pocket aces, won a three-way pot to reach $4,500. I stole a few blinds, then flopped a set, doubling through to $11,000.

Four hours later, I won the tournament. Miracles happen—never give up! Remember, going out in ninth place with a whimper pays exactly the same as going out ninth with a bang.

MAKING THE FINAL TABLE

You've made the prize money. Time to breathe a huge sigh of relief. Any sense of comfort may be short-lived, however, as you're likely to experience a "broken table."

As the contestants continue to get knocked out, the tournament director has to scramble to maintain an equal number of players at each of the tables. He or she will do this by breaking down an existing table, reshuffling its occupants to fill up the empty seats that dot the remaining tables. At some point (if it hasn't happened already) you're going to find yourself surrounded by a brand-new set of opponents whose tendencies and tells may be unfamiliar to you, and who, more importantly, don't know that they're supposed to be afraid of you.

Unless you're lucky enough to be pitted against some faces you recognize, it's okay to tighten up again until you've rebuilt your mental profiles. Don't wait too long, however, as there's another Bubble to exploit once you start to smell the Final Table. This is especially true if the tournament is going to be on TV.

POT COMMITMENT

As the blinds increase and the antes grow larger, the stakes—very literally—grow bigger. You are going to be put to the test, faced with decisions that could cost you all of your chips.

When faced with heavy action, it's often best to

cut loose from the hand and wait for a better opportunity. An exception to this rule would be those times when you're pot committed—you've already invested too much of your money into the middle.

Say you've re-raised an early raiser with something like half of your chips. Now he comes over the top of you, re-raising an amount that would put you all-in. What do you do?

You may be wondering how to answer a question like this without knowing what cards you are holding or how many chips you have left. The truth is that it really doesn't matter!

You are getting at least 3-to-1 odds on your money. There aren't too many situations in poker where one hand is a 3-to-1 favorite over another. The mighty A-K is only a 2-to-1 favorite to beat the lowly 7-2 (chew on that the next time you're tempted to whine about how you never win with Big Slick); the same holds true for confrontations like 10-10 vs. J-4.

While the wiser course of action is to avoid getting pot committed in the first place, once you're there, don't be afraid to go all the way!

THE FINAL TABLE

While there may be some debate over what constitutes a final table—most tables hold nine people, but the World Poker Tour has popularized the practice of waiting until they're down to six before the cameras start to roll—you'll certainly know you're there. Making a final table is one of the highlights of any poker player's career.

The Scouting Report

You try to sleep, but it's just not happening. The adrenaline is still flowing, and you can't stop thinking about what the final table will look like the next day. It's time to put that nervous energy to good use by putting together a scouting report.

Your scouting report is just a collection of all of the information you have gathered over the course of the tournament—or, in some cases, your career—about the opponents you'll be facing at the final table. Once you've determined what their strengths and weaknesses are, you can look for ways to exploit them. They play too loose before the flop? Re-raise them frequently. Too conservative? Rip off their blinds without mercy. Weak after the flop? Look for opportunities to get into more flops with them.

Here's an example of a report I put together before starting the final day at the World Poker Tour's Bay 101 Shooting Star in 2004. I was in Seat #6 with $1,230,000, over half the chips in play:

SEAT #1

$175,000 in chips. He'll still be stinging from that big bluff I put on him with eight people left and will be looking to make a "play for the cameras" against me with a bluff of his own. Money will not be an issue for him until there are three players remaining; even then, he'll care more about impressing the folks back home than winning a $75,000 prize. Bet strong hands into him, hoping to entice a bluff or semi-bluff re-raise. Check my draws behind him, killing his chance for the bluff steal. Let him hang himself.

SEAT #2

$200,000 in chips. She will be very uncomfortable in front of the cameras and either play extremely recklessly (hastening her exit from the stage) or very tight, too scared to make a big mistake. Judge her state of mind early in the going and play accordingly. The money will be very significant to her, so trade on her wanting to "move up." Her favorite move is the pre-flop-all-in-re-raise-from-the-blind, so any time I have a BIG hand when she's in the blind, I'll come in for a raise—she has yet to raise all-in into an unraised pot. She makes plenty of mistakes after the flop, pushing in with draws and underbetting good hands. Her minimum raise from late position is nearly always a steal, and she is very capable of folding a medium-strength hand for a sizable re-raise. A quick post-flop call from her signifies weakness, NOT a draw. A prolonged huddle and call is usually second pair or worse. She will move in with nearly every flush draw after huddling. Play to trap. Limp with medium pocket pairs when she's in the blind.

SEAT #3

$400,000 in chips. He's extremely happy just to be at the final table. He seems afraid of my game and will stay out of my way while I whittle down the other guys, avoiding confrontations and laying down some possible winners. That being said, he's seen me make a couple of bluffs and will be leery of being made a donkey on television. Value betting is the key to beating this guy. He has a tell, the classic "lean back" when he has a strong hand. That tell will manifest itself if I take the time to play with my chips, counting them out, etc. If he doesn't lean back after a minute or so, I can re-raise—even on a complete steal— and have a very good chance of picking up the pot.

SEAT #4

$200,000 in chips. If Seat #3 seems afraid of my game, this guy looks completely terrified. He'll do anything to avoid a confrontation with me. I will, of course, pick on his blinds without mercy. If he raises from the button, I can smooth call in the blind and lead at the pot. He will definitely be playing to "move up" and it shouldn't be too hard to steal pots from him. I didn't see enough of his play yesterday to pick up any physical tells, but he'll be very uncomfortable in front of the cameras and his mannerisms should reveal quite a bit. He doesn't talk much, so if I engage him in conversation during play he's very likely to reveal the strength of his hand.

SEAT #5

$200,000 in chips. The money will not be an issue for him. He knows that he can't outplay me and will be looking to play solid poker. He will probably play very tight and avoid being in pots with me. Every time I'm under the gun with this guy in the big blind, I should raise. I'll have to play solid poker to beat him, taking advantage of position whenever I can. When he raises from the small blind, I'll call in the big. If he checks after the flop, he'll usually have a weak hand and be willing to lay it down in the face of a bet. He's not a habitual check-raiser, usually betting his good hands after the flop. He is a shy and quiet type but won't want to appear stiff on television. The key is to engage him in banter—he'll give up information when he stops talking. Engaging him in banter will probably make him uncomfortable on camera. The key is to get him to start talking—he'll give up information when he *stops.*

Going to Battle

There's no secret to surviving a final table. You'll pretty much be doing what you've been doing all along, only with more money on the line.

Position remains incredibly important. Avoid having to play flops when you're out of position. You need to be extremely careful if someone has called your pre-flop raise behind you, or if you get a "free pass" from the blinds after someone's limped in. It's very dangerous to have someone acting behind you. Try to avoid calling raises from the blinds; it's much better to re-raise, putting your opponent to the test, or to simply toss your cards away and wait for a better spot.

You should, of course, be exploiting your own position, especially if you've uncovered any reliable indicators revealing the strength of an opponent's hand. For example, it's often profitable to **flat-call** early position raisers when you're on the button with all kinds of marginal hands if you have a pretty good sense of how they'll act if the flop misses them.

Put yourself in their shoes: Let's say they find A-K and open with a raise. You flat-call from the button with something like J-7; the blinds fold. They're already hating life, biting their nails over what kind of hand you could have called them with. About one time in three they'll flop a pair and come out firing. The other two times, however, the flop will miss them entirely and it will be very hard for them to call a decent-sized bet—after all, you had to call their raise with *something*, right?

In other words, you'll have a good chance of picking up a raised pot two out of every three times you play this way, providing a very healthy positive expectation. On your best days, the flop will come down A-7-7 and you'll have an excellent shot of ending their tournament right there.

If you're short-stacked, you can't be afraid to take a stand. Letting your opponents steal your blinds or raise you out of the pots with any consistency, and you're certainly going to lose. Look for ways to be aggressive—raise all-in, for example, to steal the blinds—and don't be afraid to call all-in bets with hands like A-K, A-Q, or pocket pairs. The key is to get your money in while you still have a chance to make a dent in your opponent's stack. Get the chips in the pot and hope to get lucky!

If you're sitting on a big stack, your goal should be to get your opponents' chips *without* giving them opportunities to double up. Remember that you don't have to win every pot against a shorter stack—just the last one. Calling an all-in bet with a marginal hand is rarely a good strategy. Let your opponents win the small pots. Eventually they're going to stick out their neck when you have the best of it. Your goal should be to grind them down slowly.

CLOSING TIME

Occasionally you'll be lucky enough to win without ever having to go heads-up against a single opponent. For example, in that Shooting Star tournament referenced earlier, I was lucky enough to take down the two other remaining players in the same hand.

Most tournaments, however, end with a *mano a mano* contest between the last two survivors. This is the moment, more than any other, when you are going to have to get lucky.

Think about it. Heads-up, very few hands are huge favorites over any other. A-K is a coin flip against any pocket pair. You are going to have to play your big hands strongly. If you get dealt pocket queens, and your opponent happens to wake up with pocket kings, it's game over. All you can do is your best to get your money into the center of the table when you have the best of it, then pray to whatever higher power, if any, you might have aligned yourself with.

Well, maybe that's not *all* you can do. At this point in the tournament, you're likely to have spent at least twenty or so hours playing with this opponent. You're bound to have picked up a few tendencies.

It's important to keep the size of your pre-flop raises consistent—you don't want to do anything that gives away the strength of your hand. While raising in position can be effective, you're also going to want to limp in from time to time as well, hopefully setting the stage for a trap situation. Raising in a heads-up situation at the end of a tournament with wired aces and coming away with only your opponent's blind qualifies as a mini-disaster.

Many good players use elements of game theory to guide their decisions at this point in the tournament. For example, you might decide that you are going to raise every time you are dealt two red cards, limp whenever they're both black, and flip an imaginary coin in your head when the suits are mixed. Applying randomizing techniques to your play makes it nearly impossible for your opponent to pick up any patterns to the way you bet.

If the flop hits you, whether a made hand or just a draw, you're going to want to play strongly. Make your opponent re-raise you with his or her better hands.

Your bets after the flop can be thought of as fact-finding missions. Your goal is to spend as little money as it takes to find out how highly your opponent values his or her hand. Whether they are conscious of it or not, each player has a *number*, an amount that will lead him to raise or fold. That number will vary from player to player, and change throughout the course of the confrontation in relation to the circumstances, but it's worth guessing at.

Perhaps above all else, heads-up poker is a contest of ebb and flow. Hands are won and lost, stacks grow and diminish, attitudes shift with each pot won. Learn to listen to the rhythm of the action, and you'll discover the opportunities to exploit it. That, plus a helping of good luck, and you'll be on your way to winning the tournament.

MAKING DEALS

Here are the players at the final table at the 2003 World Series and the prizes they took home:

1.	Chris Moneymaker	$2,500,000
2.	Sam Farha	$1,300,000
3.	Dan Harrington	$650,000
4.	Jason Lester	$440,000
5.	Tomer Benvisitsi	$320,000
6.	Amir Vahedi	$250,000
7.	Yung Pak	$200,000
8.	David Grey	$160,000
9.	David Singer	$120,000

You may notice some interesting things about the way the prize money gets distributed. The difference between eight and ninth, for example, is only $40,000, while the difference between first and second is $1.2 million. The jump from ninth to third isn't as big as the one from third to second.

Many players, realizing they're a cold run of cards or a bad beat away from a life-impacting drop-off in prize money, will attempt to negotiate a more favorable split. Deal-making has long been a part of tournament tradition.* They can be struck any time after the Bubble, occasionally even *on* the Bubble—it's not uncommon for the remaining players in a tournament to agree on a redistribution of the purse, extending the number of places to be paid.

Most deals, however, take place at the final table. The survivors compare the sizes of their stacks and negotiate a split of the prize money, generally based on some mutually agreeable estimate of each player's chances of taking

* It may not be for much longer. The World Poker Tour recently banned deal-making from all of its events.

first place. Sometimes formulas are used. When heads-up, for example, both players will often agree to take second-place money, splitting the rest as a ratio of their current chip counts.

These formulas tend to be fluid, as the parties negotiate changes to the terms and conditions based on intangibles, like level of skill or propensity for luck. It's been reported that when he found himself heads-up against wily pro Sam Farha, Chris Moneymaker, a relative amateur, offered to split the remaining prize money 50/50, despite having twice as many chips at the time. Farha, perhaps a little too confident in his abilities, refused the deal. The decision cost him more than a half-million dollars.

Then again, it's not easy to make that kind of decision when there's a still a tournament full of adrenaline and emotional drama ahead of you. When offered a deal, you're generally better off letting someone else—preferably a trusted friend with a head for numbers and a calculator—do the negotiating for you.

♥ ♦ ♣ ♠ ♥ ♦ ♣ ♠ ♥ ♦ ♣ ♠ ♥ ♦ ♣ ♠ ♥ ♦ ♣ ♠ ♥ ♦ ♣ ♠

YOUR DEFINING MOMENT

Structure:	**No Limit Hold'em Tournament, ninety-minute rounds**
Blinds:	**$800-1,600, $200 ante**
Your Stack:	**$90,000 ($50,000 average)**
Players Remaining:	**80, 27 places paid**

You've been playing great poker for almost two solid days in the Commerce Casino's $10,000 World Poker Tour event. You have the respect of the table, as you have rarely shown down a loser. There are three weak players remaining at your table, each with about $40,000. Unfortunately, the guy on your right is not one of them.

This serious, young, intelligent pro is well known and is playing very good poker. Besides you, he's the best at the table by far, and he isn't afraid to make aggressive attempts to steal the blinds. You, however, aren't afraid of aggression, and in the last couple of hours have re-raised what you judged to be steal attempts on three separate occasions. Two of those times you actually had a hand; the third time you were attempting a "re-steal" of your own. The Young Pro laid down his hand all three times.

A new hand. All fold to the Young Pro, who makes his standard raise—about two and a half times the size of the big blind—from the button, about $4,000 of his $60,000 stack. You squeeze your cards just enough to see that you have J♣ J♦ . Your heart races as you declare, "Raise." With a steady hand, you push $14,000 into the center of the table. The pot is just over $22,000.

The big blind folds, and the action moves back to the Young Pro. He pauses, about fifteen seconds or so, then announces without inflection, "All-in."

What do you do?

♥ ♦ ♣ ♠ ♥ ♦ ♣ ♠ ♥ ♦ ♣ ♠ ♥ ♦ ♣ ♠ ♥ ♦ ♣ ♠ ♥ ♦ ♣ ♠

THE ANSWER

What a fine mess you've gotten yourself into, yet again. You have $76,000 in chips. There is a little more than $77,000 in the pot, and it will cost you about $46,000 to call.

If you call and win the pot, you'll have more than $150,000, making you the tournament chip leader. Call and lose, you'll feel the pain, but still have a serviceable $30,000 stack. Fold, and you'll still have your $76,000, about 50 percent more than the average stack in the tournament.

Putting mathematics aside, let's think about the hand from a psychological perspective.

Here are the factors that might lead you to call:

- You have pocket jacks, a very good hand against most holdings.

- You are getting about 1.7-to-1 odds on your money, and have to win the pot only around 37% of the time ($46,000/$150,000) to make the call worthwhile.

- You have re-raised his late position raise three times in the last few hours—he may think you are on a steal and has decided to take a stand with a less-than-premium hand.

Here are the items working against you:

- The Young Pro has an above-average stack and has no reason to commit all of his chips at this point in the tournament.

- At the moment of his re-raise, he had only $4,000 invested in the pot.

- Jacks are a strong hand, but a huge underdog to the kinds of hands people like to raise all-in with, namely pocket aces, kings, and queens. Even against ace-king, you are only a slight favorite.

- You can't be sure, but you suspect he thinks you're a good player. He has been very patient most of the day, and there is plenty of easier money at the table.

The more you think about this hand, the more your jacks are looking like seven-deuce offsuit. Calling off a significant portion of your stack at this stage of the tournament with a hand that could very well be utterly dominated is just plain silly. If the Young Pro has made an amazing bluff, or is just willing to risk his entire stack on a virtual coin-flip with ace-king, well, hats off.

You fold.

Your opponent tosses 10-2 offsuit faceup into the muck as the pot gets pushed his way. "What did you have, jacks?"

You offer a noncommittal shrug by way of reply as he continues: "I knew you had to lay down that hand. I couldn't have run that bluff if you weren't such a good player."

You nod and give him the respect deserved by a fantastic read . . . and the balls that allowed him to follow through on his instincts. The weaker players at the table shift restlessly in their seats. They know that they are going to have a hell of a time beating you when you're playing so well.

11

PLAY POKER, QUIT WORK, AND SLEEP TILL NOON!

In his book of the same name, John Fox, a veteran of the California draw scene that was so vibrant in the 1970s, argued that the most profitable time to play poker was between three and six in the morning, especially the last fifteen minutes, when, as the casinos neared closing, the bleary-eyed losers would make their frantic efforts to get unstuck.

Nowadays, many cardrooms stay open twenty-four hours, and it's not uncommon to meet a player who is working on his second or third day of play, perhaps having retired to a nearby hotel room for a shower. Or not.

Watching the World Poker Tour on TV, it's easy to think

that poker is a glamorous way to exist outside the system. For the professional player, it's often anything but. Poker is an awfully hard way to make an easy living.

THE SOCIAL ANIMAL

Layne Flack seems to have it all. He's young, has an easy charm, and—as one of poker's rising stars—has earned a lot of prize money. How's your personal life, Layne?

"What personal life?"

The job requires odd hours, and a lot of them. Mike Matusow, another young, funny guy who just might be the best pot-limit Omaha player in the world (just ask him and he'll tell you about it . . . for ten minutes), claims it's almost impossible for a poker player to have a girlfriend. "Women don't understand it when you say that you'll be home by 10 P.M., then you come home at 10 P.M.—the next night—because you're stuck. At least they know you're not cheating on them. They know exactly where to find you."

"Poker is very analytical and forces you to hold things close to your vest," says Chris "Jesus" Ferguson. "Sometimes that carries over into your personal life." Ted Forrest, the consummate Vegas poker pro, once played for *five* straight days and nights. That's a 120-hour session, if you're counting.

Poker is a very social game, as long as you don't mind socializing with a tired, drunk, and unshaven lot who'd like nothing more than to separate you from your money. Certainly not an ideal situation for the discovery of a soul mate, life partner, or even a one-night stand.

"I think I spend too much time playing poker," confesses John Juanda, another young poker millionaire. "I'd like to spend more time with my family."

Some bring their family with them. Joy Cloutier, wife to the legendary T. J., almost always accompanies her husband on the road. Others make poker players out of their family, like Howard Lederer, who famously taught his sister Annie Duke the fundamentals of playing cards for a living. Still others make a family out of poker players. Jennifer Harman, for one, recently married fellow rounder Marco Traniello.

And at least in one regard, the life is getting easier—the rise of televised poker has conferred a celebrity status on some of its champions. Cloutier has been recognized around the world, in places as unlikely as the Chunnel connecting England to France. Ferguson admits that fame has helped him to overcome his shyness: "People come up and talk to me . . . I love it!" Antonio Esfandieri, reveling in the glow of a recent magazine profile (not to mention a few televised tournament wins), brags that the game has helped his "baby vig" to skyrocket:

"It used to not be cool to be a poker player. Now it's cool to be a poker player. . . . And sometimes when you're at a bar and you're talking to a girl, someone comes up to you and goes, 'Hey, you're that guy' . . ."

GRINDERS

Returning once again to *Rounders,* you might recall that Mike McDermott learned what he knew from Joey Knish, played by John Turturro. "I tell you to play within your means, you risk your whole bankroll. Not to overextend yourself, to rebuild—you go into hock for more. I was giving you a living, Mike. Showing you the playbook I put together off my own beats."

Knish is the consummate poker "grinder," a dedicated player who ekes out a living by being just a little bit better—and a lot more careful—than his competition. Despite what you might think, it's not a particularly exciting way to make a living. "I'm not playing for the thrill of fucking victory," Knish admits. "I owe rent, alimony, child support. I play for money. My kids eat."

A professional poker player's gold standard has traditionally been to earn a big blind or two every hour. In the ultracompetitive games played at poker's higher limits, that goal might be restated as a half, or even a tenth of a blind. Think about that the next time, after steamrolling over the competition at the $3/6 table, you start to think about playing poker for a living.

Then again, a tenth of a big blind in a $2,000/4,000 game is nothing to sneeze at.

Playing poker for a living requires a ferocious amount of discipline. Good players don't make many mistakes. Great players will go several sessions without making one at all. When your edge in a game is a fraction of a bet an hour, there's not a lot of wiggle room.

Perhaps even more important to the profession is

bankroll management. The road to success is littered with broken players who failed to account for the gut-wrenching roller coaster ride statisticians call "variance." As Chris Ferguson is fond of pointing out, luck is, by definition, streaky. It's not as uncommon as you might think, for example, to lose one hundred hands in a row, or to have pocket kings cracked ten consecutive times.

Conventional wisdom dictates that a professional player should maintain a bankroll some 400 times the size of the big bet in the game he or she is playing. That's probably a little low. If you're playing $10/20 poker for a living, your roll shouldn't dip below $8,000.

Keep in mind that your playing bankroll is exactly that. Your living expenses—which should probably include health insurance and retirement savings—will come from whatever you can make in additional winnings. Some months you'll make plenty, others you will make very little, if anything at all. And yes, there are losing months. To put it in context, imagine a traditional job that required you, after a tough week, to pay your employers.

Don't forget that the taxes on gambling winnings can be extremely high, often pushing 50 percent. It's one of the reasons so many gamblers move to Nevada—aside from the endless action and cheap housing, there's no state income tax.

PROPS

Don't look now, but the player sitting next to you might be employed by the casino. Many brick-and-mortar card-rooms—and an increasing number online—employ **props** (short for "proposition players") to sit in their games. It's not a nefarious scheme to milk more money out of you, except to the extent that you wind up playing more hands. The job of a proposition player is simply to keep alive a casino's otherwise shorthanded games.

It's not a glamorous job. There aren't always employee benefits. They generally don't get to choose the games they play in, and they have to switch tables if the casino wants to apply their efforts elsewhere. They are often prohibited from revealing the nature of their occupation to any of their fellow players.

Some are paid an hourly wage; others receive a small sum for every hand they play. While no official records are kept, there is certainly anecdotal evidence to suggest that propping can be a lucrative way to make a living. A long-time prop at Hollywood Park was recently investigated by the IRS, who suspected that he had failed to pay taxes on some $8 million in earnings.

If you are considering making poker a career, finding service as a prop may be a way to ease the transition. Talk to the floorman at your local cardroom, or root through the various online cardrooms, especially the new ones that are looking for players to fill their virtual seats.

STRESS, HEALTH, AND "LIFE LEAKS"

You would think that regularly suffering through the whims of cruel fate would create a breed of stressed-out, quivering husks barely resembling human beings.

Spend some time with professional poker players, and it often seems like the exact opposite is true. While not quite at the level of, say, Buddhist monks, most top players seem incredibly relaxed, especially for people who, in any given day, will experience bankroll swings in the five and six figures.

There's nothing inherently relaxing about playing professional poker; rather, the people playing professional poker have figured out a way to relax. It's simple survival. Stress leads to lousy poker. Those who can handle it survive. Those who can't, well, they find another line of work.

Of course, the way someone handles stress can often come with its own set of problems. While some poker players are workout fanatics, many more are not. Days, months, years of sitting at a table isn't quite what the surgeon general recommends. Jack "Treetop" Strauss, 1982's World Series champ, died of a heart attack at the table a couple of years later. (His cards were turned over, as the legend goes, revealing one last bluff.) Obesity among players is common, as are the measures to combat it—at least the less strenuous ones, like liposuction and stomach stapling.

Others are inveterate gamblers. Brilliant men and women who are models of discipline and self-restraint at the poker table think nothing of wagering huge sums of money on a round of golf, a presidential election, or a bit of trivia.* Sports gambling is another temptation: "There's a reason," observes Amarillo Slim Preston, "why the casinos always put their poker rooms next to the sport books." There are more than a few instances of great poker players making a huge score in a tournament, only

* During a high-stakes poker game at the Bellagio, Mike Matusow once bet—and lost—$5,000 to Howard Lederer in a debate over whether or not *The Shawshank Redemption* won the Best Picture Oscar the year it was released. (It did.) What made the wager particularly painful for Matusow was that he ignored a warning from Doyle Brunson, who had already lost the same bet to Lederer.

to lose it all a couple of hours later at a craps or blackjack table.

In other words, being a professional poker player isn't just about playing poker. You have to shore up not only the leaks in your game, but those in your life as well.

AIRPLANE GAMES

Traveling the tournament trail means spending lots of time in cars, airplanes, and restaurants. And waiting on line for cars, airplanes, and restaurants. What may seem like enforced downtime, however, is actually a great opportunity to hone your poker skills. Here are a couple of two-player games that require only a deck of cards and a scratchpad to keep score. Warning: Engaging in these games can put a serious dent in one's bankroll well before a poker table is ever reached.

Negotiation Poker
Each player is dealt two cards, then take turns trying to "negotiate" a deal, i.e., "I'll let you lay down your hand for $2." If no deal can be struck, the case goes to "arbitration"—five community cards. The player with the best hold'em hand wins; the loser has to pay the winner $5.

"Lenny's Delight"
Named for Tiltboy Lenny Augustine, this game combines the play of hold'em with the card-counting skills of blackjack. One player acts as the House, the other is the Player.

Two cards are dealt face down to each. The Player then has the option of discarding his hand, paying $2 to the House. If he decides to play, the House turns up his two cards, then deals five community cards. Whoever loses has to pay the other $5. The House then uses the remaining cards to deal another two hands, and the game is repeated. Once the entire deck has been used up, the players swap roles and start again.

THE TOURNAMENT TRAIL

Attend a major tournament, and you'll quickly identify an easy camaraderie among the regular players. Cheerful greetings are exchanged. There's gossip — "I heard that so-and-so is stuck like $2 mil" — ribbing, and practical jokes. It's a little bit like getting to go to summer camp every three weeks. That is, if having a successful camp experience was necessary to your very survival.

There used to be a distinction between the people who played high-stakes cash games and those who entered tournaments. Today it's hard to find a big-time player who doesn't play tournaments — the prize pools have grown too large, and poker's surging popularity has created an influx of dead money that shows no signs of slowing down.

In some ways, the swelling number of participants has made winning tournaments more difficult. If you are playing extremely well, you're going to be getting your money into the middle when you have the best of it. Let's say that you consistently find yourself with a 2-to-1 edge over your opponents. Even with those odds, it's going to require a lot of luck to survive confrontations against three hundred opponents. Expand that field to 2,576, the number of people who played in the 2004 World Series of Poker, and you're going to have to withstand four times as many challenges. Daunting odds indeed, especially when you consider how many players have adopted a "ram and jam" style of moving all-in at virtually any point in the tournament, increasing the number of times that you are going to have to put your entire stack at risk.

The overpopulation problem is alleviated, of course, by the exponentially higher payoffs. Greg Raymer, winner of the 2004 World Series, took home $5 million. You don't have to emerge victorious in too many tournaments to call it a career.

For the first time in poker's long history, there's serious discussion about corporate sponsorship, potentially sucking even more money into the system. It hasn't taken off yet, but it seems to be only a matter of time.

Many successful players are themselves mini-poker corporations. Some pre-sell "pieces" of themselves before a tournament, subsidizing the entry fees. Nor is it uncommon for poker players to swap pieces among themselves, an insurance policy to help alleviate the sting of an early tournament exit.

If you're planning to hit the tournament trail, here are a couple of tips:

BE SOCIAL

Getting to know your fellow players isn't just being a good neighbor; it's being a good businessperson. There's nothing wrong, for example, with wining and dining experienced players in exchange for tips on how to play an opponent whose game is unfamiliar to you.

STAY WHERE YOU PLAY

Tournament breaks aren't very long. If you've got a hotel room in the casino where you're playing, however, you can turn an hour-long break into a nap, a room service meal, or a little time to zone out in front of the TV.

CONTINUE YOUR EDUCATION

You may think that you've outgrown all of the poker books in your library, but there's always room to improve. One way is to find a poker mentor, preferably someone who is better and more experienced than you are. A mentor can help you find weaknesses in your game, betting patterns, tells, even attitudes that need adjustment.

There are also some excellent resources on the Web to improve your game. The RGP newsgroup and the message boards at Two Plus Two (*www.twoplustwo.com*) and United Poker Forum (*www.unitedpokerforum.com*) are great places to discuss strategy, especially the play of specific hands. World Poker Tour winner Andy Bloch runs a good forum at *www.wptfan.com*. And the Full Tilt Poker Web site, *www.fulltiltpoker.com*, allows you to e-mail your favorite player with questions about your play.

THE FINAL WORD

Roy West, *Cardplayer* magazine columnist and author of a great book on seven-card stud, once wrote the following advice to would-be professional poker players:

> *"You have exactly two chances: slim and none. If that discourages you, you should be discouraged and give up all thought of being a poker pro. But if being shown your chances just makes you want it all the more—if your desire to be a professional poker player is equaled by your desire to breathe air into your lungs after struggling to the surface from a deep dive—go for it. That's the kind of desire it takes."*

Or as Mike Matusow observes: "Anyone who says it's a great life is full of shit. It's an up-and-down, manic-depressive existence. I question it every day," adding, "Then again, it made me a millionaire."

THE MAJORS

As of 2004, these are the most prestigious tournaments in the poker world.

THE WORLD SERIES OF POKER

Binion's Horseshoe, Las Vegas, Nevada

The granddaddy of them all. So big, we've devoted the next chapter to it.

THE WORLD POKER TOUR CHAMPIONSHIP

The Bellagio, Las Vegas, Nevada

While 2004 was only its second year, the $25,000 entry fee—far and away the highest among major tournaments—lends instant credibility to the climax of the World Poker Tour's season.

GRAND PRIX DE PARIS

The Aviation Club de France, Paris, France

The only European stop on the World Poker Tour takes place each July in this elegant cardroom that's been spreading games for nearly one hundred years.

LEGENDS OF POKER

The Bicycle Club, Bell Gardens, California

Each July, players from all over the world descend on this famed Los Angeles cardroom for a month of tournaments with a prize pool in the millions.

BORGATA POKER OPEN

Borgata Hotel Casino and Spa, Atlantic City, New Jersey

The new kid on the boardwalk, this September tournament is quickly becoming one of poker's most prestigious.

ULTIMATE POKER CLASSIC

Playa Linda Beach Resort, Oranjestad, Aruba

Sponsored by poker site UltimateBet.com, it's hard to beat the setting. Plus the chance to put a face on players with online handles like "Peasant," "Ticker," and "Krazy Kanuck."

WORLD POKER FINALS

Foxwoods Casino, Mashantucket, Connecticut

More city than casino, Foxwoods hosts this $10,000 buy-in tournament each November.

FIVE DIAMOND WORLD POKER CLASSIC

The Bellagio, Las Vegas, Nevada

The Bellagio's "less prestigious" tournament, held each December, boasts a first-prize purse of over $1,000,000.

POKERSTARS CARIBBEAN ADVENTURE

The Caribbean Sea

Whatever your feelings about cruise ships, it's hard to resist the idea of a weeklong jaunt through the Caribbean in the middle of January with a guaranteed prize pool in the millions.

JACK BINION WORLD POKER OPEN

Horseshoe Casino/Goldstrike Casino, Tunica, Mississippi

The spirit of the riverboat gamblers lives on each January in this multimillion-dollar tournament hosted by Benny Binion's son.

THE L.A. POKER CLASSIC

Commerce Casino, City of Commerce, California

This California institution, the biggest poker room in the world, hosts one of the biggest poker tournaments in the world each February.

BAY 101 SHOOTING STAR

Bay 101, San Jose, California

High-stakes poker comes to northern California each March, where in 2004 a guy named Phil Gordon took home first place and $360,000.

PARTYPOKER.COM MILLION

The Pacific Ocean

Each April, another online poker site, another cruise, another multimillion-dollar prize pool. Ho hum.

WORLD POKER CHALLENGE

Reno Hilton, Reno, Nevada

Players flock to the Sierra Nevada mountains each March to bring in the spring and vie for millions in prize money.

YOUR DEFINING MOMENT

Are you ready to go pro?

There is no official certification that denotes your status as a professional. There are no diplomas, no Bar exams, and certainly no one who will be there for you if you fail. To go pro, you need confidence, experience, and the ability to answer an honest "yes" to each of the statements that follow. Notice that in each case, there is not a "no" box. If you're answering "no" you don't go pro. Period.

❏ YES. I have amassed at least 1,000 hours at the table at the limit I will be playing the majority of the time. During that time period, I have won an average of at least one big bet per hour at that limit and below. I am a winning player with experience.

❑ YES. I keep excellent records, including all time spent at the table, the limits, the name of the floorman, and my net win/loss for each session. I resist the urge to forget losses or overstate wins. The numbers that I write down are the same numbers that I tell my significant other, unless of course, that significant other is in the habit of going to Armani the day after a big win or withholding sex after a big loss.

❑ YES. I am playing big enough to support my desired lifestyle. If I need to make $60,000 a year, I'm playing at least at the $15/30 level and winning at least one big bet per hour at the table. I am playing big enough stakes.

❑ YES. I have an adequate bankroll. I have at least 500 big bets in my poker bankroll and 4-6 months of living expenses money completely separate from my poker money. I have enough money.

❑ YES. I avoid lending money to or bankrolling other players, even those with really great sob stories or annoying persistence. I realize that a not so insignificant number of these loans will forever go unpaid. My bankroll is, well, my bankroll. My money is under my control.

❑ YES. I avoid negative expectation gambling with my bankroll at all cost. I don't shoot craps after a big win, I don't bet on a sports "lock." And I certainly don't play keno unless the keno runner is extremely good looking and wears extremely revealing clothing.

❑ YES. There are people in poker who play a much better game than I do. I understand that this game takes a lifetime to master and I am always willing to learn from those who play better. I am a winning player, but a player who learns when there is something to be learned. My ego is in check, or at least a little bit smaller than Phil Hellmuth Jr.'s.

❑ YES. I look around the table and constantly reevaluate if I should be sitting at that table. I am capable of getting up and leaving the casino if conditions so warrant, no matter if I'm winning or losing. I can leave a great game to make a dinner date with my significant other and not feel bad about it. I have excellent table selection skills and discipline.

❏ YES. I am capable of folding 1,000 hands in a row if it is right to do so. I wait for a good table instead of sitting down in a negative expectation game. I have patience.

❏ YES. I have a friend or group of friends in poker to whom I can turn for advice. These friends respect my game but will give it to me straight. They are better players than I am, and they are willing to help me reach the next level. I have poker mentors.

❏ YES. I take good care of myself. I do my best to eat right, sleep right, and maintain my health. I don't play when I'm sick, depressed, or upset. When I go to the poker room, I go in as a well-rested, healthy professional ready to win. I have good enough health to perform.

❏ YES. I am capable of playing my best game no matter what the stakes. Even if I'm used to playing $30/60, I can play my best game at $10/20, $5/10, or even $3/6. I can separate the stakes of the game from the correct way to play the game. I play the game well no matter what is at stake.

❏ YES. When I play my best game, I feel just as good about a losing session as I do a winning session. I know that the poker game is not defined by a single session, but is just one long winding road. I am emotionally stable.

❏ YES. I love playing the game. I love thinking about the game. I dream about the game. I strive to be the best player I can be. This is something, above all else, that I want to do. I am a poker player . . . a professional poker player.

12

THE WORLD SERIES OF POKER

It's been called the most American of games, but it's played in nearly every corner of the world. Walk into any cardroom and you'll see that great melting pot in action, people of all ages, sexes, ethnicities, and socioeconomic backgrounds competing in an arena where none of those distinctions matter. It can be a family game played for nickels and dimes, or a high-stakes battle as intensely competitive as any physical sport, but you'll (almost) never see a fight escalate beyond a few angry words. It combines brains with bravado, patience with aggression, hope with despair.

It's poker.

Unless you've been living in a cave all your life, you're already familiar with the game. At the time of this writing, there are three regularly scheduled poker TV shows on the air, with several more in development. A search on Amazon.com for poker books and related merchandise returns more than 16,000 selections. Online poker sites are growing like kudzu, making it possible to find a game with someone, somewhere in the world, at any time of day or night.

Thirty or forty years ago, poker was relegated to what T. J. Cloutier calls "the backrooms"—pool halls, hotel rooms, brothels, or anywhere else a game, usually shady, often dangerous, could be spread away from the prying eyes of the law.

Today, players compete for massive prizes in televised tournaments. Immensely skilled professionals vie for five-, even six-figure pots in ultra-high-stakes ring games. The top poker players are multimillionaires. One particularly successful pro—who will remain nameless lest we tip off the IRS—grossed some $10 million last year alone. Several, including Cloutier, have become celebrities and are recognized all over the world.

While money is generally the measure of a poker player's success, the game's highest honors are still awarded at the World Series of Poker, a series of tournaments held annually at Binion's Horseshoe in downtown Las Vegas. The final event is the most prestigious, the $10,000 buy-in no-limit hold'em championship. It's among the most grueling title events in any sport or pastime, usually requiring fourteen hours of poker—for as many as seven consecutive days—to crown the winner. The lucky player has not only become an instant multimillionaire, but can, at least for a year, lay claim to being the world's poker champion.

• • •

In 1969, Benny Binion accepted an invitation from his old friend Tom Moore, who had just purchased the Holiday Hotel in Reno, to attend an event to mark its grand reopening. The "Texas Gamblers Reunion" brought together some of the most famous road gamblers from that state—including Amarillo Slim Preston, Texas Dolly Brunson, and Jack "Treetop" Strauss—with a few non-Texans as well, like pool hustler Rudolph "Minnesota Fats" Wanderone and oddsmaker Jimmy "the Greek" Snyder. They played poker, attracting a surprisingly large number of spectators.

Benny Binion was impressed. The following year, he attempted to duplicate the success of the Reunion with his own event at the Horseshoe, which he dubbed "The World Series of Poker." Thirty-eight men gathered in a small room that was normally reserved for baccarat and played five different poker games. Johnny Moss, the Texas legend who had broken Nick "the Greek" Dandalos at the Horseshoe some twenty years earlier, was voted the best all-around player by his peers and awarded a trophy.

Hoping to generate more publicity, Binion altered the format the following year, transforming the event into a winner-take-all "freeze-out." Six players coughed up a $5,000 entry fee and began to play. The ending was hardly surprising—Johnny Moss broke all five of his opponents to win his second consecutive title.

In 1972, despite doubling the size of the entry fee to $10,000 (a figure that has remained the same ever since) the tournament grew to eight players. Then to thirteen, prompting Binion to boast to an interviewer, "It's liable to get up to fifty, might get up to be more than that."

He lived long enough to see Phil Hellmuth, in 1989, defeat a field of 178 to become the youngest champion in the tournament's history.

In 2004, Greg Raymer outlasted 2,575 opponents to win the gold bracelet (the jewelry was added to the winner's spoils in 1974) and $5 million in cash. More than 3,500 players are expected to participate in 2005.

The World Series, as the name suggests, is actually a train of almost forty poker tournaments, beginning with a $500 buy-in limit hold'em contest for Las Vegas casino employees. Over the course of the next month and a half, champions are crowned in Omaha hi-lo, lowball draw, and several variants of seven-card stud. An event called "S.H.O.E." combines four different games: Stud, Hold'em, Omaha, and Stud Eight-or-Better. There is a tournament for senior citizens, and another just for the ladies. The final and most prestigious event of all, however, remains the No-limit Hold'em World Championship.

It's nearly impossible to describe the rush of adrenaline that flows through your veins when the tournament director announces the start of the contest: "Shuffle up and deal!" The atmosphere resembles a carnival. There are celebrities (a trend started by Gabe Kaplan, TV's Mr. Kotter, who has been playing since the late '70s). Some players wear costumes. Nearly every recognizable professional in the world is in attendance.

The battle goes on for seven grueling days, each around fourteen hours long. When two players are left, the prize money—millions in wrapped stacks of hundred-dollar bills—gets dumped on the table, adding even more drama to what has already been an event riddled with mind-boggling highs and lows.

Nearly every professional poker player (and an increasing number of amateurs) aspires to win the title of World Champion. It's been won by some of the world's greatest—Moss, Brunson, Ungar, Chan—and a few names that, before the final showdown, had never been heard before, instant celebrities like Moneymaker and Robert Varkonyi.

GETTING IN

What separates the World Series of Poker from every other sporting event, aside from the prize, is its inherent democracy. You can shoot free throws all year long, or spend hour after hour in a batting cage, but you'll never get the chance to fight for position against Shaquille O'Neal with an NBA title on the line, or face Mariano Rivera, with two outs in the bottom of the ninth, in Game Seven.

Plunk down ten grand, however, and moments later you may find yourself seated at a table with T. J. Cloutier, Doyle Brunson, and Amarillo Slim Preston, vying for a gold bracelet.

Nowadays, the $10,000 isn't even a requirement. Satellites have been held since 1983, allowing a lucky player to win a seat at a tenth of the cost. If $1,000 still sounds too extravagant, you can try your hand at one of a myriad of supersatellites offered by local cardrooms and online poker sites around the world. Chris Moneymaker's road to riches began with a $40 entry at PokerStars.com.

With practice, thought, and luck, you can do the same.

WHAT IT FEELS LIKE

PART I: THE BITTERSWEET
SAGA OF RAFE FURST

My best friend and fellow Tiltboy, Rafe Furst, is a very good poker player.

He should be—he's been playing since he was twelve years old. In 2001, wizened by ten years of solid post-collegiate play, he decided to take a shot at the World Series. After winning a seat in a single-table satellite the night before the big event, Furst went on to play four days of very solid poker. He didn't win any prize money, but managed to place fifty-seventh out of 615, a very respectable showing for the first time out.

The second year didn't go as well, as he suffered through two days of horrendous cards before getting knocked out. There was no bang, just a lot of slow, painful whimpering. But he felt like he had done the best he could given the hands he'd been dealt, and he cast an optimistic eye toward his next try.

He didn't have time to play a satellite in 2003, but the now-veteran Furst felt good enough about his chances to plunk down the full $10,000 entry fee. He took his seat amidst a group of strangers, briefly noting two empty seats, and began to play. After only a couple of hands, it became clear to Furst that he was, in all likelihood, the strongest player at the table. A perfect situation, he thought, to play the role of table captain, aggressively pushing around the opposition. After only one orbit, he had increased the size of his stack by about ten percent.

That's when the latecomers arrived. The two empty

seats were filled by John Juanda and Layne Flack, who are not only two of the best no-limit hold'em artists in the world, but players notorious for entering lots of pots and manipulating them with frightening aggression. Juanda in particular had posed problems for Furst in the past, having knocked him out of several other tournaments, and was probably the last person in the world he wanted to face, especially at the first table.

No need to panic. I'll just need to be careful about picking my spots.

As fate would have it, that spot came a couple of hands later, as he looked down to find a pair of tens in the hole. With everyone passing in front of him, Rafe opened with a decent-sized raise. Everyone folded—that is, except Juanda, who smooth-called the raise from the blind.

The flop was an A-Q-10 rainbow, not ideal, but pretty close to it: a set of tens for Furst, and the chance to force Juanda to make some very critical decisions, should he be holding an ace.

Juanda bet $1,000. A probing bet. *He's looking for information. Well, let me give him some.* Furst raised $4,000.

"All-in!" Juanda cried, without hesitation, pushing his chips into the center of the table.

The next two minutes were agonizing, as Furst considered all of Juanda's possible holdings. *Could he have been setting a trap with pocket aces? Did he flop a straight? Or is he making a move on me, knowing that I'll be too intimidated to risk this many chips so early in the tournament?*

This is the World Series of Poker. These are the kinds of decisions that you have to make, correctly, for a week of fourteen-hour days. Get one wrong, and you're going home.

Furst finally decided that Juanda was holding an ace. *Maybe he's got two aces, and I'm beat, but if he's making a move with A-K or A-Q, I've got him dead to rights.* "I call."

Juanda didn't bother to hesitate, turning over pocket queens, a larger set that left Furst with only one card in the deck—the fourth ten—that could bring him salvation. It didn't come. In less than five minutes, Furst had gone from table captain to a shipwrecked survivor, barely clinging onto his tournament life. *I have $1,200 left.* It occurred to him that this was the exact amount that Phil Hellmuth, Jr. had battled back from in 2001 to place fifth. *Time to hunker down.*

The previous year he had played for two days without seeing a premium hand. This year, two hands later, Furst looked down to find A-K. *No reason to get fancy here.* He made the standard raise and—*yes!*—this time Juanda folded. Layne Flack, however, proved less cooperative. "Raise," he declared, after looking at his cards in the big blind. "All-in."

Unlike the previous hand, Furst didn't have to think about this decision—there was too much money in the pot and too little in front of him to do anything but call.

Flack turned over pocket jacks, setting up a classic coin-flip scenario.* The board failed to produce an ace or a king, Flack took the pot and Furst . . . well, he earned the distinction of, after only two circuits around the table, being the first player to get knocked out of the 2003 World Series.

It wasn't a lack of experience, or extraordinarily bad

---

* Well, not *exactly* a coin flip—the jacks are about a 57-43 favorite here, but it's a close enough decision for Furst's call to be an easy one.

play, it was just the way the cards fell during those first few hands.

PART II: THE PHIL AND I

Everyone who is familiar with professional poker has heard of Phil Hellmuth Jr. To know Phil is, in diplomatic terms, to have an opinion of him. He can be brilliant one moment, then in the next display a level of emotional maturity that would be embarrassing to most three-year-olds. In other words, he's a perfect candidate to put on tilt.

Hellmuth began his day at 2001's final table in great shape, virtually tied with Carlos Mortensen for second chip position. I, the other Phil, was lucky enough to be there in the middle of the pack, not such a bad position either.

If you've played against Hellmuth, you've likely been subjected to a battery of pre-flop raises. He's an aggressive player who isn't afraid to use his stack (and reputation) to steal your blinds. While putting together my scouting report the night before, I decided the best way to combat his style of play would be to push all-in against him the first time he tried it, regardless of the cards I'd been dealt. Not only would it make poker sense but, if successful, I knew I'd have a pretty good chance of putting him on tilt—I had, after all, listed my occupation as "Professional Tiltboy."

It didn't take long for my plan to become a reality. The fourth hand of the tournament, I was in the big blind. Hellmuth came in for a decent-sized raise and I immediately called "all-in." Hellmuth thought about it for a time, then made what he deemed to be the professional course of action given my show of strength—he folded.

"I guess I'd better look at my cards," I said, looking down for the first time at my Q-2 offsuit. I shared the discovery with Hellmuth. "You ran over me yesterday, but you are not going to do that today." While his lips curled into a smile, something in his demeanor suggested that he didn't find it as funny as I did.

The play struck a resonant chord with a few of the other players at the table, as two more of Hellmuth's raises were met with monster re-raises, leading the former World Champion to muck his hand each time.

So when, a few hands later, Dewey Tomko came over the top of his fourth attempt at a raise, Hellmuth decided to make a stand with A-Q, a strong but easily overrated hand, as it's a significant underdog to most of the premium hands players tend to raise all their chips with. Like A-K, which, coincidentally, happened to be the very hand that Dewey Tomko had raised all his chips with. Big Slick held up, and, as we took our first break, Phil had gone from third-from-first to third-from-last.

My second chance to teeter Hellmuth came shortly after the second break, when I trumped his latest raise by moving all-in with pocket 6s. Hellmuth immediately called me with his pocket 9s, the same hand he had won the 1989 WSOP with, a hand that was nearly a 5-to-1 favorite to beat mine. Had I made a terrible mistake, or was I simply demonstrating mastery over the concept of Implied Tilt Odds? Clearly I had screwed up—Big Time. But the powers that be were looking after me, and my big underdog hand came through: I flopped a third six for my set, delivering a crippling bad beat that sent Hellmuth a little higher up the Tiltmeter.

A couple of hours later, Hellmuth was still stinging from the beat. I could see it in his subtle facial expressions, his posture . . . but mostly in the way that he wouldn't stop talking about it. As fate would have it, we found ourselves together again in an unraised four-way pot with Carlos Mortensen and Stan Schrier. The 4♠ Q♥ 9♦ flop did nothing for my hand, and I quickly folded to Hellmuth's $60,000 raise, a decision I appreciated even more after Mortensen re-raised $200,000. Schrier took a little longer to fold—he was a bit embarrassed, as he later admitted, that he had spaced out for the full two minutes it took him to act—perhaps giving Hellmuth a little too much time to dwell on his hand in his altered state of tiltedness. He re-raised Mortensen all-in with his Q-10, an uncharacteristically weak hand for him to make such a strong play.

After a few minutes (it seemed like an eternity), Mortensen called him with Q-J. A jack on the turn gave Hellmuth, who was holding Q-10, an open-ended straight draw and a glimmer of hope, but an ace on the river ended his tournament. As poker writer Andy Glazer observed of Phil's quick exit from the room, "He didn't explode. I think it was more of an implosion."

It wasn't meant to be my day either. After Phil was eliminated, I think I let down my guard a bit. Just fifteen minutes later, I made a huge blunder and ran into Carlos Mortensen's monster hand, pocket queens. I ended up finishing fourth. Even so, a fourth-place finish—and the nearly $400,000 that accompanied it—offered plenty in terms of consolation.

♥ ♦ ♣ ♠ ♥ ♦ ♣ ♠ ♥ ♦ ♣ ♠ ♥ ♦ ♣ ♠ ♥ ♦ ♣ ♠ ♥ ♦ ♣ ♠

SIX DEFINING MOMENTS

It's the granddaddy of them all, the World Series of Poker. You've been playing excellent, solid, aggressive poker throughout the preliminary events, managing three final tables and more than $80,000 in prize money. After your entry fees and expenses, you're up a cool $45,000. The $10,000 entry fee doesn't faze you. You're ready to become the next world champion, your picture permanently enshrined on the Wall of Champions right there in the Horseshoe poker room. All you have to do is outlast 1,199 players.

Start of Day One
Your stack: $10,000. Average stack:
$10,000. 1,200 players remaining.

DAY ONE

Throughout the early going, you've been following your tournament strategy to perfection. You've gained a little ground, turning your initial $10,000 stake into $12,500 without a showdown. You're playing tight, aggressive poker, and all the players at the table know it.

The blinds in the third level are $75-$150. You're in late position, two away from the button, and you're dealt one of those hands that you absolutely love — pocket eights. You decide that winning the blinds just isn't worth a lot right now, and that you would rather sacrifice a little bit of pre-flop equity for the chance at a really big pot. You limp and call the $150 blind, hoping to catch one of the small and big blinds—Internet supersatellite winners—for a lot of chips.

The small blind shrugs his shoulders and calls, and then the big blind thinks a bit and raises it up another $500. You're not too happy about this turn of events, but eyeing the big prize—the big blind's remaining $5,500—you don't mind investing another $500, especially as you're fairly confident the small blind will fold, leaving you heads up and in superior position.

You try to breathe normally and concentrate on your opponent when the flop is dealt. You notice his marked sign of relief as the flop comes J-8-2 rainbow. You immediately put him on an overpair to the flop, Q-Q or K-K. What he doesn't know is that you hit your gin card.

The opponent bets right out, $800. You need to form a plan for extracting the most money possible. Call, slowplay, or raise? If you decide to raise, how much? Think!

DAY ONE ANSWER

Clearly, you should raise. There are too many scare cards that can come on the turn that will shut your opponent down. An ace or a jack, for example, and you're not likely to win very much more money. If you raise now, your opponent will probably put you on A-J or K-J and will very likely re-raise all-in.

You raise $1,700 to $2,500 total, putting your opponent in a real bind. . . . Are you on a pair of jacks with A-J? K-J? Q-J? J-10? If so, he should re-raise you all-in. It's almost impossible for him to lay his hand down here, and, sure enough, after a minute or so, he re-raises all-in. You, of course, beat him to the pot. He turns over K-K, drawing to two outs. The turn and river bring an ace (which would have killed your action had you merely called). Justice is served, and you've busted your opponent out of the tournament. Your stack has grown to $18,650. Well played.

End of Day 1
Your stack: $28,500. Average stack:
$24,000. 500 players remaining.

DAY TWO

Sleep doesn't come easily, but you know that you're in top form. You head down to the tournament room about thirty minutes early to check out the composition of your table. You're slightly alarmed to find that the two players you fear the most in the world, Phil Ivey and Howard Lederer, are seated to your left, each with more than $40,000 in chips. This is going to be a very long, tiring day.

After several hours of play, the blinds are at $500-$1,000, with the average stack somewhere near the $40,000 mark. You've had it rough, but you've managed to do okay, building your stack to $29,000. There's an hour to go before the much-needed break and the change in tables that accompanies it.

You're in middle position and you pick up American Airlines, A-A, a very welcome sight. The early position players fold to you. You, of course, decide to come in for a standard-size raise, $3,000 to go—no time to get fancy here, with Lederer and Ivey and their huge stacks left to act. Lederer folds, the small blind folds, and you're just about to rake in the blinds when Phil Ivey raises to $8,000. He has $85,000 in chips remaining. Your play, your Defining Moment.

DAY TWO ANSWER

Well, you have a few choices really. You can re-raise all-in, or call and hope to trap Phil for more betting after the flop.

Re-raising all-in makes a lot of sense here, while trying to trap Phil Ivey out of position is just asking for trouble. There is $8,500 in the pot, and if you can take that right now, you'll be just about average and, with just under an hour to go, in great shape to survive with enough ammunition to face a (hopefully) easier table tomorrow.

So, you re-raise all-in. Ivey sits back in his chair and shakes his head. After about thirty seconds, he calls and flips up K-K. Not even the great Phil Ivey could get away from that hand here. Whatever worries you had disappear after the flop comes A-5-5. Well done, and due to some great timing, you're now up over $58,000 and in great shape. If you had just called, of course, Ivey would have put you on A-K and, after that flop, would have refused to put another red cent into the pot.

End of Day 2
Your stack: $53,500. Average stack: $54,500. 220 players remaining.

DAY THREE

You slept surprisingly well, with only a few nightmares involving Chris "Jesus" Ferguson and Erick Lindgren. But, for some reason you can't quite remember, you woke up at 6 A.M. in a cold sweat screaming "Jen!"—Jennifer Harman, no doubt. You can't possibly get back to sleep, so after a quick shower, you head down to the tournament room to check out the seating assignments. Lo and behold, Jennifer Harman is on your left. You look further down your list and find Annie Duke, who has about $75,000 in chips, on your right. Under different circumstances, being sandwiched between these two would be a fantasy come true. But this is Day Three of the World Series of Poker. You have your work cut out for you. Again.

You are cautiously optimistic when the day begins. The blinds are $800-$1,600, with a $200 ante. Aside from the two ladies, the rest of your table doesn't seem that tough. You vow to wait patiently for a hand, using the time to concentrate very hard on your opponents, hoping to pick up tells.

Well, that's the plan, anyway. You wind up on the receiving end of some good hands accompanied by very bad luck. Twice you pick up two red queens and raise, get called by the button, and twice, to your utter dismay, the flop has come A-K-7 with three spades. You (correctly) lay your hand each time. Another time, after a short stack of $8,000 raises from late position, you look down to find A-K suited in the big blind. You raise him all-in, of course. He calls you with pocket twos—a fishy play for sure—but he survives and you take a beating. And finally, in an even bigger tragedy, you get Jennifer Harman all-in for $14,000 after you flopped a set, only to have her make a runner-runner flush to double up.

Long story short, your well-above-average stack at the start of the day has evaporated. You're down to $18,000, a very short stack given that the blinds are $1,000-$2,000, with a $200 ante. You vow not to tilt, but it is very difficult to maintain your composure. Another hour passes, you steal a few blinds, but you can't seem to get above that $18,000 hump. The blinds are increasing in fifteen minutes, if you last that long.

You are in the small blind. Everyone folds to an aggressive player in middle position with an average stack, who ups it to $6,000, his standard raise. Annie Duke thinks for about sixteen seconds before deciding to call from the button. You notice that the initial raiser leans forward in his chair when Annie calls. You look down at your cards — pocket sevens.

Your play, your Defining Moment.

DAY THREE ANSWER

You have three viable options: call, raise, or fold. There are merits to each. You quickly weigh them in your mind:

Call: If you flop a seven, you will very likely double if not triple up. If the flop looks too scary, you can lay your hand down and still have $12,000. If the flop comes low, you can move all-in and hope you have the best hand.

Fold: You'll still have $18,000, you'll have the button, and you'll likely get in another full round before the blinds go up again. You're on a short stack, but at least you're in. You might be able to find a situation better than this one to get all-in.

Raise: You may pick up the pot — a not-so-insignificant $16,800 — and nearly double up without a showdown. If you do get called, you still may have the best hand, although it is unlikely to be a huge favorite. You are a 4.5-to-1 underdog to a pocket pair better than yours. But at least you'll have three ways to win: everyone may fold, you may have the best hand, or you may suck out a win even if you don't.

You think more carefully about Annie's hand. Unless she's trapping with a huge hand — aces or kings — she likely has an ace with a big kicker. She probably would have re-raised with A-K, making A-Q most likely, maybe A-J or A-10. She might have a pocket pair like jacks, tens, nines, or eights and be reluctant to re-raise, a play you've seen her make many times.

What kind of hand could the initial raiser have? Your thoughts go back to the "lean forward" after Annie's call. He seemed concerned—a sign of weakness. He probably doesn't have a big pair, or even A-K. His most likely hand, you think, is A-Q.

Finally, you focus on your own image. Despite the recent run of bad luck, you're not steaming, although your opponents will probably think that you are. They've seen your stack disintegrate. They know that you're hurting and will have to make a move. You finally decide that, should you move all-in, at least one of them is going to call you.

Man, what a close decision. If your read is correct, however, and they both have A-Q, they will be drawing slimmer than normal—your 55 percent chance of winning actually soars to 64 percent. Better to err on the side of aggression, you decide. "All-in."

Your opponent asks for a count of your remaining chips. This is a good sign—at least he doesn't have aces or kings. After the count, he looks a little uncomfortable but ultimately decides to call. Annie looks unhappy, but folds her 8-8 faceup. Whew! A good decision by her, but a great decision for you. Your opponent turns up A-Q, just as you thought. Now, just survive the flop . . .

It's a good one for you, 3-4-6 rainbow. You're feeling very confident, but your heart sinks as the dealer peels off a Q. Your opponent cheers in jubilation, your friends gather round and pat your back. You rise and gather your jacket. The dealer pauses, the air seems to thin, you can feel the pounding in your head. The crowd gasps, and you see a beautiful sight—a red 5 in the middle of the table, giving you the straight, the win, and $45,000 in chips. You're still below average with some work to do, but you're back in action!

The rest of the day goes very well for you. You play solid poker, trusting your instincts to make some great reads, rebuilding your stack to $140,000. You're not too disappointed when Jennifer busts out, nor when Annie gets a call from the baby-sitter with the news that one of her kids is puking. She has to leave the tournament with only two players left on the Bubble, leaving you with a table ripe for stealing. You win seven pots in a row before the day comes to an end, and you take your stack all the way up to $245,000. At the end of Day Three, you find yourself in thirtieth place, a guaranteed payday. At the top of the leaderboard? Phil Hellmuth Jr., of course, surrounded by a massive $592,000 in checks and thirty-nine reporters vying for sound bites and interviews.

End of Day 3
Your stack: $245,000. Average stack:
$222,000. Fifty-four players remaining.

DAY FOUR

This is likely to be the longest day in your poker life. With fifty-four players remaining, you anticipate fifteen hours of play to get down to the final nine. The Starbucks triple espresso helps to wipe away the cobwebs. You feel confident and ready for action.

Besides Phil Hellmuth Jr., Phil Ivey, Howard Lederer, Chris Ferguson, Amir Vahedi, and John Juanda are all still alive. The other forty-six—including you—are largely unknown. But you're making a great name for yourself. Your poker mentors hover near the rail, offering their support and well-wishes. Tournament director Matt Savage calls out his favorite phrase, "$3,000-$6,000 blinds, $500 ante, shuffle up and deal."

With $13,500 in each pot before the flop, stealing blinds will be of paramount importance. But just as important, because most of the pros think you're a fish, you need to establish a very tight image. Your stack gives you the luxury of waiting for a hand, and you do just that for over an hour. You fold A-J suited under the gun. You toss away pocket tens from second position. Maybe you're playing too tight, but you've definitely got the image you're going for. When you finally do come in for a raise, you'll get some respect.

After ninety minutes of folding hand after hand, you exploit your tight image to steal two sets of blinds from late position, then another on each of the subsequent two rounds. When the blinds go up to $4,000-$8,000, you find yourself pretty much exactly where you started. The better news is that, in the interim, six more players have been eliminated.

The next three hours are a blur. You get some good hands, but no one plays back at you. You bust a short stack, and then are forced to retreat from a few steal attempts after you've re-raised, but in general, you're in control. Thirty-five players remain.

The blinds are $6,000-$12,000 with a $2,000 ante.

You've got $320,000, just below the average of $340,000, when you pick up a promising hand on the button.

The hyperaggressive player on your right, who seems to have been involved in five pots every rotation, comes in for a raise of $26,000. You sense weakness as you examine your own cards, 7♦ 6♦. You definitely don't think you have the best hand, but you're pretty sure you can take the pot right here with a re-raise and aggressively pop it to $60,000. The small blind folds, the big blind goes into a long and pronounced huddle before finally doing the same. Despite your hopes and prayers, however, Hyperaggressive Guy, who has about $420,000 in chips, decides to call the $60,000. You are going to see a flop for the first time in what feels like days.

The flop comes 9♦ 7♠ 5♦. All things considered, a fantastic flop for this hand. There is more than $140,000 in the pot. Your opponent checks to you. Despite all of your concentration, you can't pick up any tells on the guy. Check or bet—what do you do?

DAY FOUR ANSWER

You run through your opponent's possible hands. Pocket jacks or tens, maybe even kings or queens. A-K and A-Q are also possibilities. Remember, he raised then called a big re-raise out of position. You have to give the guy credit for a hand.

With a pair and a flush draw, you're a slight favorite against nearly all of those hands, so it wouldn't be totally insane to go all-in right here and now. You'd certainly have to think about calling if he moved all-in on you. If you were to make a smaller bet, like $50,000, you'd be pot committed if he were then to re-raise you all-in.

How about checking? Fourteen cards—any diamond, any six or seven—will make your hand worth moving all-in on the turn. That's almost a third of the cards left in the deck. Maybe you should check and see what comes next . . .

You finally decide that the rewards for getting your opponent to throw away a hand like A-K are too great to ignore. You gather your courage and you move all-in. Hyperaggressive Guy sits up in his chair, winks to the crowd, and turns over two black aces. "Gotcha!" he says.

Even the dealer, a longtime friend, looks concerned. But no worries, mate. The most beautiful card in the deck—the four of diamonds—comes off on the turn. Hyperaggressive Guy collapses on the floor in agony. As you gather the chips and confirm that you are still, in fact, capable of breathing, you somehow resist the temptation to tell him that you were a 53 percent favorite after the flop. You took your shot and got lucky. You have to do that at least once in a tournament to win. Well done. Now, get up from the table, take a short walk, and think about how good life is. You're one of the chip leaders in the World Series of Poker, with only forty-four people left.

You have fuzzy memories of the mayhem that ensued after an unknown Canadian Internet player, Krazy-something-or-other, got knocked out in tenth place. He raised under the gun, inspiring chip-leader Phil Hellmuth Jr. to move him all-in for his remaining $300,000. Phil turned over his favorite hand—pocket nines. The Canuck couldn't turn his cards over fast enough, two red kings. The flop brought three rags, the turn a queen, and the river, that fateful river, showed a nine. The Canuck promptly slid back from the table, shook everyone's hand, threw his chair through the window overlooking Fremont Street, and became the first player in the history of the tournament to exit Binion's from the second story.

The good news: You have made the final table at the World Series of Poker. The bad news: Phil Hellmuth Jr., with $2,350,000, holds a dominating chip lead.

End of Day 4
Your stack: $990,000. Average stack:
$1,333,000. Nine players remaining.

DAY FIVE

You're a little below average in seventh chip position, but still have plenty of fight and play. After the obligatory interviews and a handful of Advil, you try to calm yourself, concentrate, and prepare for the battle ahead. Only eight players stand between you and immortality.

Seat 1: Phil Ivey, $1,780,000

Seat 2: Phil Hellmuth Jr., $2,350,000

Seat 3: John "the in-over-his-head Internet dude" Doe, $550,000.

Seat 4: Clonie "I'm the only woman at this table" Gowan, $600,000

Seat 5: Tom "super-tight" Jones, $1,400,000

Seat 6: Howard Lederer, $1,600,000

Seat 7: "Briz," $1,530,000 and twenty-three pounds of gold chains around his neck

Seat 8: Some guy reading this book and playing great poker, a.k.a. you, $990,000

Seat 9: Mr. Online Qualifier, "MonkeyBars69," $1,200,000

Your friends and family (and a few of your creditors—word travels fast) are gathered behind you in the bleachers. This is the big one, the time for you to shine.

Your strategy is to sit back, relax, and let your tight, aggressive play do the talking. You are going to pick on the average-sized stacks, avoid mixing it up with Ivey, Lederer, and Hellmuth, and wait for the weaker players to make critical mistakes.

"Shuffle up and deal!" The blinds are $10,000-$20,000 with a $2,000 ante. You are in the **cutoff**—the seat just to the right of the button—and on the very first hand pick up a monster: ace-king suited. Your heart rate speeds to 180 beats per minute and you feel like you might actually explode.

Hellmuth looks down at his cards in first position and raises to $70,000. A nervous Clonie Gowan calls from middle position. Briz, seated just to your right, thinks for a minute before calling as well. What the hell is going on?

You know that Hellmuth could be playing just about anything right now. He's the chip leader, probably wants to send a message on the first hand, and doesn't need a big hand to raise under the gun. Clonie, the short-stack, can't have a great hand—she would have re-raised Hellmuth if she did. Same logic applies to Briz, who surely would have stabbed at the nearly $200,000 in the middle were he sitting on a big hand. You decide to make a huge play, a monster move, and shove 'em all-in.

A hush falls over the table. Hellmuth stares you down for a good two minutes, but when he doesn't call in the first fifteen seconds you know he's going to lay his hand down. Clonie looks very unhappy and folds. Briz fingers his gold for about a minute before tossing 6-6 faceup into the muck. A euphoric sense of calmness and control takes over your body and mind as you stack your new pile of chips.

Clonie goes out in the first hour, followed shortly after by Tom Jones. John the Internet Dude gets eliminated in the third hour. The only "easy money" left at the table is MonkeyBars69 and maybe Briz, although he's playing his A-game. You've won your fair share of the cash, however, and are well above average with six players remaining.

Seat 1: Phil Ivey, $1,600,000

Seat 2: Phil Hellmuth Jr., $3,300,000

Seat 6: Howard Lederer, $1,800,000

Seat 7: Briz, $2,100,000

Seat 8: You, $2,500,000

Seat 9: MonkeyBars69, $1,300,000

The blinds are now $15,000-$30,000, with a $5,000 ante—that's $75,000 in the pot even before anyone's had a chance to look at his cards. You're in the cutoff again, Ivey and Hellmuth in the blinds. After Lederer and Briz fold, you look down to find two little red "ducks"—pocket deuces. A minimum raise seems in order. You gather some chips and sling them into the pot, intending to raise to $65,000, but somehow you wind up with only $35,000 in your hand. (Five days of poker have taken their toll.) You offer a weak protest, but tournament director Matt Savage won't hear it. No string bets allowed. He gives you back one of your $5,000 chips. You have just limped in late position. Live with it.

The button, MonkeyBars, eyes you suspiciously before calling. Ivey calls what is only an extra $15,000 from the small blind. Hellmuth shrugs and says, "Let's see a flop."

K♥ 5♠ 4♠ hits the felt, and Ivey and Hellmuth check. It's on you. You decide that the chances of getting check-raised are too high, and you check. MonkeyBars checks behind you, somewhat quickly, you observe. You are done with the hand.

Until the turn brings a glorious, fantastic, unbelievable card—the deuce of clubs. Ivey and Hellmuth check once again. With $140,000 in the pot, you decide that you have to bet, as it's too easy for one of them to have a three and a straight draw. The two spades pose a problem as well, but you can't believe that Ivey or Hellmuth would have checked twice with four cards to a flush. MonkeyBars69, however . . . You bet $100,000, a nice intimidating number, enough to give anyone on a draw the worst of it.

MonkeyBars69 leans back in his chair, contemplates, and then raises to $300,000. Ivey and Hellmuth quickly exit. It's on you. This is your Defining Moment.

FINAL TABLE ANSWER

What in the world is going on? Okay, it's time for a thorough analysis. You call for time and begin to replay the hand in your head.

Would MonkeyBars have slowplayed a king on the flop? Not with a spade draw threatening the board. He would have bet at least half the pot. He doesn't have a king. You're sure of that.

How about a set of fours or fives? God, could this really be possible? Could he have checked the flop with a set, against the three of us, in spite of the spade draw? Yes, it's possible, for sure, but something about this theory doesn't feel quite right. He'd surely be worried about a player like Ivey or Hellmuth getting a free card on the turn. You think he'd bet at least a little bit after the flop, hoping like hell to get raised by a king or a flush draw. No, a set doesn't seem right.

What does that leave us with? A medium pocket pair, like sevens or eights? If he doesn't think you have a king, it's a definite possibility. Pocket threes? A raise to $300,000 with the open-ended straight draw would be a great play here, one that he's capable of.

How about A-3 suited? Ouch. That *really* looks like a possibility. The relatively small raise seems to indicate that he *wants* to get called. You remember that he leaned back in his chair after the deuce hit the board—usually an indicator of strength. The more you think about it, the more you worry about the straight. You decide that this hand is just about as likely as any medium pocket pair.

What to do, what to do. Raising all-in seems like a very bad play. You will only get called if he has you beat with a bigger set or the made straight. A small re-raise, say $600,000, won't help you much either—if he re-raises you all-in, you'll likely be pot committed to call.

You can't raise, but you know you shouldn't fold. That leaves one option: call. And you do. Your opponent ever-so-slightly shakes his head.

You hold your breath and wait for the river: Q♦. There is a little more than $700,000 in the pot; your opponent has a little less than a million in front of him. Your play, and your second Defining Moment on the same hand.

FINAL TABLE ANSWER FOLLOW-UP

Well, folks, that shake of the head did it—definitely an indicator of strength. You have a set, a fantastic hand, yes, but sometimes you can smell a rat. This is one of those times. Still, this is no seasoned pro you're up against, but a guy who qualified online. Maybe, just maybe, he's getting out of line, misjudging the strength of his own hand. You could be holding the best cards.

There is only one way to know for sure, and that is to make a bet on the river. Something that he can call with a hand that's worse than yours, but not large enough to destroy your stack should you have to cut bait.

You decide that $250,000 seems about right, count out the chips and slide them into the pot. His voice is meek, but there's no hesitation as MonkeyBars calls out the words you dreaded: "I'm all-in."

Shit.

Well, at least now you know you're beat. You muck your hand, of course, and MonkeyBars shows the entire table the A-3. "What'd you have?" he asks.

"Not much," you fib. "A busted flush draw and gutshot straight draw."

"Yeah, that's what I put you on," he says.

"You really had a flush draw?" It's Hellmuth, taking the opportunity to needle you from the other side of the table. "What a fishy way to play that hand. What was that, $250,000 on the river? Did you really think you could buy it for $250,000?"

You try, but you can't resist. "Actually, *Phil,* I turned a set and laid it down."

"You didn't have a set. No way *you* could lay down a set."

The cameras are rolling. You reach into the muck and pluck out your ducks. "Set of deuces."

Hellmuth goes pale. Lederer smiles, Ivey stands up. You see a look of admiration in Briz, reflecting off his bling. MonkeyBars looks at the chips you have left in front of you—*his* chips—and looks like he might start to cry.

The crowd erupts into thunderous applause. This is your table now. You own these guys.

The next four hours fly by. You wield your newfound authority with supreme confidence, stealing blinds, playing position with perfection. You bust Ivey—Phil Ivey!—then get sweet revenge against MonkeyBars, flopping another set of twos against his pocket queens. Meanwhile, Hellmuth knocks out Lederer. When Briz finally gets "blinded" off, you find yourself heads-up against you-know-who: Mr. Hellmuth.

Your stack: $8,000,000. Hellmuth Jr.: $4,000,000.

HEADS-UP

Like a dream, the box of money—over $5 million in neatly wrapped stacks of hundreds—gets dumped on the table. There is hardly any room for the chips. The winner will get $3,250,000, the runner-up $1,750,000. This is absolute nirvana.

The roar of the crowd has finally dulled into a low murmur. Okay, focus. You have twice as many chips as your opponent. You are going to make history.

The blinds are $50,000-$100,000 with a $20,000 ante. Hellmuth has the button, and after due deliberation, he raises to $350,000, making it $250,000 to call. You control your urge to throw up and squeeze your cards, discovering K♣ J♣ —a suited "Kojack."

You are clearly going to play this hand. Raising will send a clear message that you are in control and that you plan to use your chip lead. Then again, it's the very first hand. You decide to call. There is $740,000 in the pot.

Matt Savage calls out the flop to the now-hushed crowd: "Ten of clubs, nine of spades, seven of hearts."

Well, you have a double-bellybuster straight draw, as any queen or eight will make your hand. You can check, hoping for a cheap draw, or you can come out betting, maybe picking the pot up right here. You decide that betting is preferable, but how much? Somewhere near the size of the pot seems right, and you fire $700,000 into the middle. "It's $700,000 to call," announces Savage, "for Mr. Hellmuth."

Hellmuth zips up his jacket. "Seven hundred thousand, eh? Why so much? You're supposed to bet $300,000 with your 9-8. . . . $700,000." You, of course, aren't saying a word, although you're fairly certain he can hear your heart pounding its way out of your chest. "Seven hundred thousand . . ."

After what seems like ten years but is actually—you later confirm watching ESPN—only a minute, Phil announces confidently, even *cockily*, "Well, I'm all-in."

It's $2,930,000 to call. You knew it would come, and here it is—*the* Defining Moment.

Your play.

HEADS-UP ANSWER

Will you call, giving Hellmuth a 2-to-1 chip lead on you if you lose? Or can you let it go, retaining a small 7-to-5 edge?

First, your outs. It's very likely that any queen or eight will give you the best hand. Recalling the *rule of four*, you know that those eight outs give you about a 32 percent chance of winning, assuming Hellmuth doesn't have one of your cards. There's also about a 6 percent chance of a runner-runner flush.

What could Hellmuth have? Here are some of his likely hands and your approximate chances of beating them:

A set of tens, nines, or sevens: 27 percent

Two pair:	34 percent
Ace-ten:	52 percent
Jack-eight:	26 percent
Pocket jacks:	38 percent
Pocket queens:	36 percent
Pocket kings:	35 percent
Pocket aces:	37 percent
King-jack:	52 percent if he's unsuited, 50 percent if he's suited with spades or hearts

It will cost you $2,930,000 to call, with the chance to win a pot containing $8,000,000. Divide $2,930,000 by $8,000,000 to get your pot odds—you'll need a 37 percent chance of winning to justify your call. You're doing okay against the big pocket pairs—great against a hand like ace-ten—but taking the worst of it if he's flopped a set or straight.

On the other hand, this could end the tournament right here. Lights. Cameras. Letterman. A sunglasses endorsement deal with Oakley. And a suckout victory against Hellmuth.

You recall hearing Chris Ferguson say that he won the

2000 Championship gambling with a worse hand against
T. J. Cloutier, as he felt it was the only way he was going
to bust the better player. And while you're not quite willing to admit that Phil is a better player—at least not in
public . . .

you call.

The entire building shrieks. Hellmuth, in a victorious
pose, rolls over his favorite hand, the hand he won this
very event with in 1989—pocket nines. He's flopped the
set. The seventeen people in the audience related to
Hellmuth cheer wildly.

You roll over your hand. "Well, at least I'm not drawing
dead!" Photos are snapping. Your mom is crying. Your sister, who read Hellmuth for the set and would definitely
have checked and folded after the flop, shakes her head in
disgust.

The turn, the hideous turn, brings the nine of clubs.
You are disgusted. You realize your pants are partially
soiled. The crowd emits what can only be described as a
collective sigh of grief. Your sister won't look at you. Matt
Savage announces, "Phil Hellmuth has four nines. But
there is still an out. The queen of clubs will make a
straight flush!"

"That only happens in movies," you say to the cameras,
your lower lip quivering.

The dealer burns.

Everything seems to be happening in slow motion.

And, as you've probably already figured out because
we're near the end of the book, the river brings that beautiful lady, the miraculous queen of clubs. You have rivered
a straight flush. You are more than $3,000,000 richer and

the champion of the World Series of Poker. You have put
Phil Hellmuth Jr. in the psychiatric ward at Las Vegas
General. You are immortal.

Congratulations.

THE LAST WORD

Making the final table at the World Series of Poker is an experience I will never forget. I dream about it often and still cringe when I think of the bad play I made to get myself eliminated. Every single minute of every tournament I enter, I am thinking about how I can improve and get back to that final table. When you get there, I think you will agree that it is the most incredible feeling any poker player can have. With some luck and skill, you could be the next World Champion of Poker. Your picture will hang next to the greats of the game.

Moss
Slim
Texas Dolly
Chan

Ungar

Hellmuth Jr.

Ferguson

Moneymaker

<Your name here>

Get out there, in the cardrooms and online. Play. Fail. Learn. Improve. Succeed. If we are ever at the same table, please say hello and then sit back, play your best game, and beat the hell out of me. I'll enjoy seeing you play well and having a good time with the game that I love so much.

Remember, your bankroll, like Rome, won't be built in a day. Start small. Take your time. Use each and every hand you play to learn. Think about the game. Dream about the game. Read everything you can about the game. Find a mentor. Play. And play more.

I sincerely hope we meet at a final table someday soon.

GLOSSARY

add-on The extra helping of chips, purchased with "regular" money, available during the early stages of some tournaments.

aggressive The natural inclination to bet or raise, a hallmark of most winning poker players. The opposite of **passive.**

all-in The ability to call a bet with whatever you have left in front of you (as opposed to, say, the deed to the family ranch).

ante The money contributed to a pot, usually by all the players at a table, before the cards are dealt.

ATM An inexperienced or just terrible poker Player who distributes money like a cash machine. See also: **fish, donor, pigeon.**

backdoor flush In Texas Hold'em, a flush completed by running cards on the **turn** and the **river.**

bad beat An agonizing loss that defies the laws of logic and/or probability.

bad beat story The ensuing tale about just how bad a beat you were delivered, generally of interest only to the teller.

big bet (**BB**) The largest bet that can be made in a **structured-limit** game, usually exclusive to the **turn** and the **river.**

big blind   A mandatory **small bet** posted before the cards are dealt, usually by the player two seats the left of the dealer.

Big Slick   Ace-king, one of hold'em's most powerful hands when it connects with the **board**; perhaps it's most frustrating when it doesn't.

blind   A mandatory bet posted before the cards are dealt, intended to create a pot worth contesting. The term also refers to the player sitting in the blind position. See **small blind** and **big blind.**

board   In Texas Hold'em, the five community cards shared by the entire table. Can also refer to the registration area in a cardroom.

board texture   The general "feel" of the community cards, allowing an observant player to get a sense of what hands his or her opponents might be holding.

boat   A full house (see Chapter Two).

bottom pair   When a **hole card** pairs with the lowest card on the **board.** A weak hand in a full game, but a powerful holding when playing **short-handed.**

Bubble   The critical moment in a tournament where outlasting a handful of opponents will get you into the prize money, final table, etc.

button   The seat occupied by the **dealer,** or the player who gets to act last during each round of post-flop betting. Also refers to the plastic disk used to mark this position in a cardroom.

buy-in   The amount of money required to sit down to a ring game or tournament.

calling station   A player easily exploited for his or her exaggerated tendency to call too many bets.

cap   The maximum number of bets that can be made on any given street, usually four or five.

case   Four of a kind.

cash machine   See **ATM.**

cold call   The act of calling multiple bets, i.e., a raise and a re-raise, in one fell swoop.

connectors   Two consecutive cards in the **hole,** i.e., 7-6, increasing the odds of making a straight.

crying call   The act of calling a bet despite the near-certainty that your hand is a loser. A common response to a **bad beat** or **suckout.**

cutoff   The seat just to the right of the **button.**

dead money   The aggregate of inferior players who have little to no chance of actually winning.

dealer   See **button.**

death card   A **turn** or **river** card that seems likely to complete a multitude of different hands for the players still in the pot.

donor   See **ATM.**

double belly-buster   A straight draw that isn't open-ended, but can still be completed by two different cards. (See Chapter Three for an example.)

doubling up   A won pot that doubles your current **stack,** the desired result of pushing **all-in** in a tournament.

drawing dead   The act of pursuing a **drawing hand,** unaware that even if you make it, you're still going to lose.

drawing hand   A hand that's not quite there yet, but could be should the right card or cards fall.

expected value   The profit or loss that a certain strategy or game will generate, on average, over the long run.

Fancy Play Syndrome (FPS)   An expensive tendency, especially evident in players who have just read Sklansky and Malmuth, to overuse "trick" plays like check-raising or semi-bluffing.

fifth street   In Texas Hold'em, the fifth and final community card, commonly known as the **river.**

fish See **ATM.**

flat-call   The act of merely calling a raise, usually from a superior position. Also called a **smooth call.**

floorman The casino employee responsible for keeping the games moving and the disputes arbitrated.

flop In Texas Hold'em, the first three community cards, dealt simultaneously.

fourth street In Texas Hold'em, the fourth community card, commonly known as the **turn**.

freeroll The opportunity to play a tournament without, for any number of reasons, having to pay for it with actual cash.

game theory The science of decision making, especially in the face of imperfect information.

gut-shot A straight draw that can only be completed by one card in the middle. Also called a belly-buster.

hand selection The notion, ignored by many new or undisciplined poker players, that certain hands are more profitable than others.

heads-up The moment when only two players remain to contest a hand and/or game.

hole cards The two "hidden" cards dealt to each player.

host The casino employee responsible for managing the flow of new players.

hourly rate The average amount a player can expect to make every hour, over the long run, from a certain game or opponent.

implied pot odds A calculation of **pot odds** based not on the money that's currently in the pot, but the total money you anticipate will be in the pot at the end of the hand.

implied tilt odds (ITO) The scientific measure of the odds that an otherwise horrible decision will cause your opponent to explode in a fit of irrational rage.

junk A hand that, at least according to the poker mathematicians, should never be played. Also called **rags**.

kicker The second card in the hole that isn't used to make your hand, but might come into play to break a tie.

kill pot In some cardrooms, a forced bet before the deal required of a player who has won two or more pots in a row.

leak An often repeated and ultimately expensive error, whether at the poker table (e.g., overusing a certain play) or in one's life (e.g., overusing the nearby sports book).

limp To enter a pot before the **flop** without raising.

loose The willingness to see flops with a wider than average assortment of hands. The opposite of **tight**.

monster A very powerful hand.

muck The pile of discards in the center of the table; also, the act of tossing your hand into said pile.

no-limit A game with no maximum bet.

nuts The best possible hand, given a particular **board**.

offsuit Two **hole cards** of different suits, the opposite of **suited**.

open-ended A straight draw, consisting of four consecutive cards, that can be completed by a card on either end.

out A card that, if dealt, will improve your hand.

overbet In **no-limit** games, the act of risking more money than you should to win a relatively small pot.

overcard A card on the board that is higher than the cards in your hand, creating the potential for a pair that's better than yours.

overlay The idea that a certain percentage of your opponents, especially in a tournament, are worse than you, improving your **expected value**.

overpair A **pocket pair** bigger than the highest card on the board.

passive The natural inclination of check or call, a hallmark of many losing poker players. The opposite of **aggressive**.

pigeon See **ATM**.

pocket pair Two matched **hole cards**; also called a **wired** pair.

position Where you sit in relation to the **dealer**, determining how early or late you'll be required to act on each street.

post a blind   The act of posting a bet before the deal, generally required of a player joining a game in progress.

pot committed   The condition of having such a large percentage of your money invested in a particular pot that there's absolutely no point in folding.

pot-limit   A deceptively complex form of poker that allows players to make maximum bets up to the size of the current pot.

pot odds   The amount of money in a pot relative to the size of the bet that you're faced with.

pre-flop   The time dedicated to action before the community cards are dealt.

premium hands   The most profitable hands in hold'em, at least before the **flop** (see Chapter Three).

prop   Short for "proposition player," an individual employed by a cardroom to keep certain games alive.

rack   One hundred chips of whatever denomination the table is playing for.

rags   See **junk.**

rainbow   A **flop** containing three cards of different suits.

rake   The hosting fee taken by a cardroom, generally a small percentage of each pot.

rebuy   A feature of some tournaments allowing players who have busted out in the early stages to purchase a new starting **stack.**

river   In Texas Hold'em, the fifth and final community card, also known as **fifth street.**

rock   A **tight, passive** player who may win very much, but isn't going to lose very much either.

rule of four   The percentage chance of completing a particular hand with two cards to come can be approximated by multiplying the number of **outs** by four.

runner-runner flush   A flush completed by two "running" cards—namely the turn and the river. Also called a **backdoor flush.**

satellite   A tournament, often held at a single table, whose winner or winners earn entry to a larger tournament.

scare card   A card whose likelihood of improving or completing a particular hand drives fear into the heart of those players still in the pot.

semi-bluff   A bet or raise with a hand that, while probably not the best at the given moment, has **outs.**

set   Three of a kind. Also called **trips.**

short-handed   The condition of playing a less-than-normal number of opponents.

slowplaying   The act of playing a strong hand with a deceptive passivity on the early streets in the hopes that your opponents will make (and find the courage to bet) their second-best hands.

small bets (SB)   The smallest bet that can be made in a **structured-limit** game, generally the mandatory increment before and just after the **flop.**

small blind   A mandatory fraction of the **small bet** posted before the cards are dealt, usually by the player seated immediately to the left of the dealer.

smooth call   The act of merely calling a raise.

stack   The chips that you have in front of you.

stealing the blind   The act of raising before the **flop** with the intention of persuading the **blinds** to fold.

straddle raise   A raise made before the cards are dealt by the player seated **under the gun,** usually in the hopes of livening up a dull game.

string bet   The act of reaching into your **stack** for chips more than once during a particular bet. Illegal in most games.

structured-limit   A game whose players must be in specific increments, usually **small bets** and **big bets.**

stuck   The condition of losing, as in, "I can't make dinner, honey, I'm **stuck** three grand."

suckout   The condition (or the verb used to describe the condition) of betting and losing with what was the best hand . . . until the **river.**

suited   Two **hole cards** of the same suit, the opposite of **offsuit.**

suited connector   Two consecutive **hole cards** of the same suit, improving your chances of making straights, flushes, or straight flushes.

supersatellite   A tournament whose winner or winners gain entrance into the **satellite** for a much larger tournament.

table image   The way one is perceived by his or her opponents at the table.

tell   An action or pattern of actions that unintentionally provides information about the strength of your hand to an observant opponent.

tight   The willingness to see **flops** with a narrower than average assortment of hands. The opposite of **loose.**

trips   Three of a kind. Also called a **set.**

turn   In Texas Hold'em the fourth community card, also known as **fourth street.**

under the gun   The player who has to act first before the **flop.**

underbet   In **no-limit** games, the act of betting too little with a made hand, giving opponents the correct **pot odds** to draw for their **outs.**

wired   See **pocket pair.**

ENDNOTES

Chapter One

Johan Huizinga, *Homo Ludens,* Beacon Press, 1971, p. 1.

Much of the history of playing cards came from David Partlett's *The Oxford Guide to Card Games,* Oxford University Press, 1990.

The quotation, as well as the descriptions of the early games and players, came from Robert K. DeArment's *Knights of the Green Cloth: The Saga of the Frontier Gamblers,* University of Oklahoma Press, 1982.

The Jonathan N. Green quote came from A. Alvarez's *Poker: Bets, Bluffs, and Bad Beats,* Chronicle Books, 2001, p. 38.

The survey taken by the U.S. Playing Card Company in 1946 was referenced in David Parlett's *The Oxford Guide to Card Games*, Oxford University Press, 1990, p. 3.

Much has been written on the showdown between Moss and Dandalos, the most complete description appearing in A. Alvarez's *The Biggest Game in Town,* Chronicle Books, 1983, pp. 29-32.

David Sklansky and Mason Malmuth, *Hold'em Poker for Advanced Players,* Two Plus Two Publishing, 1988, p. 1.

The source material and quotation concerning Truman's skill

(or lack thereof) as a poker player comes from an article by Raymond H. Geselbracht entitled "Harry Truman, Poker Player," which originally appeared in *Prologue,* the quarterly from the National Archives and Records Administration, Spring 2003, Vol. 35, No. 1.

The estimate of Richard Nixon's poker winnings comes from an interview with fellow naval officer James Stewart from the WGBH program *American Experience: The Presidents,* first televised in 1990.

The quote from *Life* was actually taken from A. D. Livingston's book *Poker Strategy and Winning Play,* Lyons & Burford, Publishers, 1991, p. 68.

Doyle Brunson, *Super/System: A Course in Power Poker,* Cardoza Publishing, 1978.

Chapter Two

Albert H. Morehead, *The Complete Guide to Winning Poker,* Simon & Schuster, 1967, p. 9.

The sad tale of the Dondorf Deck came from an article by Fred Taylor entitled "The Deck That Broke a Card Factory's Back." It is cited here from *Clear the Decks,* September 1997, Volume XI, Number 3, but apparently appeared first in *Hobbies* magazine in 1960.

Chapter Three

The "Sklansky Hand Rankings" are reprinted, with the permission of the authors/publishers, from Sklansky and Malmuth's *Hold'em Poker for Advanced Players.*

The quotation from the misinformed General Robert Schenck ("The deal is of no special value") also came from A. Alvarez's *Poker: Bets, Bluffs, and Bad Beats,* p. 27.

David Sklansky, *The Theory of Poker,* Third Edition, Two Plus Two Publishing, 1999, pp. 17-18.

Lee Jones, *Winning Low-Limit Hold'em,* ConJel Co LLC, 2000.

Chapter Four

Big Julie's quote comes from A. Alvarez's *The Biggest Game in Town,* p. 52.

Mike Caro, *Caro's Book of Tells,* Mike Caro University Press, 2000.

The T. J. Cloutier quote about Bill Smith came from an interview with Dana Smith that appeared in Smith, Tom McEvoy, and Ralph Wheeler's *The Championship Table*, Cardsmith Publishing, 2003, p. 100.

Chapter Five

F. Scott Fitzgerald, *The Great Gatsby*, Reprinted Edition, Scribner, 1995, p. 5.

The Jen Harman quote comes from a segment entitled "Meet the Pros" on Ira Glass's radio show *This American Life* (Episode 192, originally aired 8/31/01).

Larry W. Phillips, *Zen and the Art of Poker*, Plume, 1999.

Amir Vahedi's quote comes from ESPN's broadcast of *The World Series of Poker 2003*.

Chip Reese's observation of Stu Ungar comes from an upcoming biography of "the Kid" by Nolan Dalla.

Chapter Seven

The description of Jimmy Fitzgerald's finery comes from Robert DeArment's *Knights of the Green Cloth*, University of Oklahoma Press, 1990, p. 24.

The description of Crandall Addington's unique sense of style comes from A. Alvarez's *Poker: Bets, Bluffs, and Bad Beats*, p. 65.

Chapter Eight

Bob Ciaffone and Jim Brier, *Middle Limit Hold'em*, published by Bob Ciaffone, 2002.

The Chris Ferguson quote comes from a personal interview.

The Dandalos quote comes from A. Alvarez's *Poker: Bets, Bluffs, and Bad Beats*, p. 97.

Chapter Nine

Anthony Holden, *Big Deal: One Year as a Professional Poker Player*, Abacus, 2002, pp. 44-45.

Amarillo Slim's observation of McManus's play comes from James McManus's *Positively Fifth Street: Murderers, Cheetahs and Binion's World Series of Poker*, Farrar, Straus, Giroux, 2003, p. 296.

The quoted portion of Rudyard Kipling's *If . . .* is, as far as the authors have been able to surmise, free of any copyright restrictions. Our humblest apologies if we are somehow in error.

Chapter Ten

The description of the debate over the format of the World Series came from *Amarillo Slim in a World Full of Fat People*, by Amarillo Slim Preston with Greg Dinkin, HarperCollins, 2003, p. 156.

The Tex Morgan quote comes from a personal interview.

The Foxwoods tournament structure was taken from About.com's section on "Casino Gambling."

Herbert O. Yardley's *The Education of a Poker Player*, Simon & Schuster, 1957, is sadly out of print.

Howard Lederer's observation of Phil Ivey's dangerous play was made on the *World Poker Tour: Foxwoods*, Season One.

Chapter Eleven

John Fox, *Play Poker, Quit Work and Sleep Till Noon!*, Bacchus, 1977.

Roy West's quotation came from "Maybe You Can Be a Professional Poker Player," one of his many excellent columns for *Cardplayer* magazine, December 20, 2002 (Volume 15, No. 26).

Chapter Twelve

The description of the "Texas Gambler's Convention" came from Slim and Dinkin's *Amarillo Slim in a World Full of Fat People*.

Binion's overly modest estimation of the future of the World Series came from Smith, McEvoy, and Wheeler's *The Championship Table*.

Phil's memory of his confrontation with "the other Phil" was assisted by Andrew Glazer's play-by-play description of "The World Series of Poker $10,000 No-Limit Hold'em Championship, Day Five," which appeared in *Cardplayer* in 2001. Glazer does not get anywhere near the recognition he deserves for his continually outstanding accounts of poker's biggest games.

Photo by Michael Hawk

Phil Gordon is the co-host of Bravo's hit show *Celebrity Poker Showdown* and a world-class poker player. He has won more than $1,200,000 in tournaments since April 2001, including two wins on the World Poker Tour and a fourth place finish in the World Series of Poker Championship event. He lives in Las Vegas. Jonathan Grotenstein is a professional poker player and freelance writer living in Los Angeles.